A Practical Prayer Guide

100 Prayers to Address Physical Ailments, Mental Distress, Emotional Turbulence, Spiritual Crises, And Modern-day Challenges | Ideal For Individuals, Families, Church Groups, and Community Leaders Facing Struggles

Preface

This comprehensive book, tailored for both the novice and the faithful, extends a hand to all touched by hardship. Whether you're grappling with physical ailments, mental distress, emotional turbulence, spiritual crises, or modern-day challenges, learn to pray and cry out to our Lord, who hears every plea. You will discover His boundless love and compassion, witness His mighty power, and feel His unwavering presence through the deepest trials.

This guide is for you, whether you're an individual seeking personal solace, a family navigating challenges together, an educator shaping young minds, a church group deepening communal faith, or a community leader striving for unity and support amidst adversity.

Introduction from the Author

My journey to these pages has been anything but ordinary. Achieving a Ph.D. by age 26 marked the onset of a path filled with both profound accomplishments and formidable challenges. At 32, I embraced the complexities of the corporate world within a Fortune 500 multinational corporation. By 37, I was navigating the turbulent waters of entrepreneurship, leading my own business toward what seemed like a worry-free horizon. Yet, beneath this veneer of success lay deep layers of personal turmoil, anguishes, and battles that tested the very fabric of human suffering.

The dissolution of two marriages transformed me into a single mother, grappling with the fading light of love and the immense responsibilities of solo parenting. Once a beacon of hope and passion, my first marriage gradually succumbed to the inevitable strains of daily life, miscommunication, and unmet expectations in eleven years. The second marriage, tainted by domestic violence and betrayal, faced further turmoil with the shocking revelation of a secret child born outside our union. This discovery prefaced a critical health condition that plunged me into a mire of despair, haunted by the fear of leaving my children unattended. I endured perimenstrual problems characterized by irregular and heavy periods for nearly five years, draining all my energy and stoking fears for my children's future. The severity of my condition necessitated an emergency room admission for a blood transfusion, underlining the critical phase of my health struggle and the pressing need for a permanent remedy. This episode was a pivotal moment in an exhaustive journey characterized by numerous diagnoses, countless specialist consultations, and a rigorous regimen of treatment trials. Each step was fraught with uncertainty, yet it was the decisive surgical intervention, coming as a conclusion to this prolonged ordeal, that brought relief and signaled the start of my recovery.

Amidst my quest for happiness, unforeseen challenges emerged. Once a source of pride and independence, my business became ensnared in a web spun by my ex-husband, leading to its abrupt closure and propelling me into a six-year legal nightmare. I faced a daunting array of legal battles: immigration issues casting a shadow over my nearly three-decade-long residency, a heart-wrenching divorce, child support disputes, a DCFS case threatening my custody, a car accident adding stress, looming personal bankruptcy, indemnity claims challenging my integrity, and a fierce criminal case defense. Each legal ordeal tested my resilience, fortifying my spirit against insurmountable odds.

In this crucible of adversity, the Lord reached out to me, transforming a stubborn heart that once revered success and scorned failure. Jeremiah 29:11 resonated deeply with me: "For I know the plans I have for you, declares the Lord, plans to prosper you and not to harm you, plans to give you hope and a future." This period of relentless trials sparked a profound spiritual awakening, teaching me the value of faith over skepticism and surrender over self-reliance.

The past decade, marked by health crises, financial upheaval, and legal fights, was compounded by the isolation of facing these battles without family support in the U.S. Yet, it was here, in the depths of hardship, that I found and forged a steadfast faith in the Lord. Christianity evolved into the foundation of my resilience and recovery, gradually steering me through the resolution of each legal challenge. In this journey, I witnessed firsthand the unfolding of God's omnipotent love and grace, guiding me to victories in custody and across the legal spectrum, affirming the profound impact of my faith in navigating and overcoming these trials.

Raising children in today's digital age added another layer to my journey. The struggles of my ADHD-diagnosed youngest son, my daughter's estrangement from faith, and my eldest son's uncertainty about his future highlight the unique challenges faced by parents today. The influence of social media on my Gen Z children has shaped their world—a world of digital connection and isolation, where values are continuously tested by the forces of social justice, mental health awareness, and cancel culture.

This book is a testament to a journey from despair to hope, defeat to faith. It is a narrative of suffering, strength, and transformation through prayer. Shared not for sympathy but as a beacon of hope, it invites you on a journey of healing and discovery in the face of life's vast challenges—physical, mental, emotional, spiritual, or uniquely modern.

As you explore these prayers, remember that you are never alone. I hope these pages will extend the same comfort, strength, and miracles I've experienced, reminding you of God's unwavering love and the transformative power of faith in overcoming adversity.

With heartfelt sincerity and unwavering faith,

Scarlett Anderson

For my three children, who inspire me every day to embody the strength, love, and grace of a devoted heart.

© [2024] by [RedQuill Impressions]
All rights reserved.

No part of this publication may be reproduced, distributed, or transmitted in any form or by any means, including photocopying, recording, or other electronic or mechanical methods, without the prior written permission of the publisher, except in the case of brief quotations embodied in critical reviews and specific other noncommercial uses permitted by copyright law.

Table of Contents

PART I: PRAYERS FOR PHYSICAL WELL-BEING

01. Acute Illnesses	3
02. Chronic Conditions	5
03. Disability	7
04. Injuries and Accidents	9
05. Hormonal Imbalances	11
06. Infectious Diseases	13
07. Reproductive Health Issues	15
08. Cancer	17
09. Nutritional Deficiencies	19
10. Inflammatory and Autoimmune Diseases	21
11. Medical Treatments	23
12. Terminal Illness	25
13 Wisdom for Healthcare Providers	27

PART II: PRAYERS FOR MENTAL RESILIENCE

14 Anxiety	31
15 Restlessness	33
16 Stress	35
17 Fear	37
18 Loneliness	39
19 Depression	41
20 Despair	43
21 Chronic Worry	45
22 Burnout	47
23 Negative Self-Image	49
24 Insecurity	51
25 Obsessive Thoughts	53
26 Compulsions	55
27 Indecisiveness	57
28 Confusion	59
29 Mental Blocks	61
30 Self-Harm	63
31 Suicidal Thoughts	65
32 Addiction	67

33 Eating Disorders	69
34 Insomnia and Sleep Disorders	71
35 Trauma	73
36 Post-Traumatic Stress Disorder (PTSD)	75
37 Attention Deficit Hyperactivity Disorder (PTSD)	77
38 Obsessive-Compulsive Disorder(OCD)	79
39 Schizophrenia	81
40 Bipolar Disorder	83
41 Psychotic Disorders	85
42 Personality Disorders	87
43 Cognitive Disorders	89
44 Neurodevelopmental Disorders	91
45 Self-Doubt and Imposter Syndrome	93
46 Body Dysmorphia	95

PART III: PRAYERS FOR EMOTIONAL WELLNESS

47 Disappointment	99
48 Rejection	101
49 Insecurity	103
50 Sorrow	105
51 Change and Uncertainty	107
52 Fears, Phobias, and the Unknown	109
53 Self-Esteem Challenges	111
54 Jealousy and Envy	113
55 Relationship Pains	115
56 Guilt and Shame	117
57 Anger and Resentment	119
58 Betrayal	121
59 Death Anxiety	123
60 Grief and Loss	125

PART IV: PRAYERS FOR SPIRITUAL CRISES

61 Doubt and Unbelief	129
62 Feeling Distant from God/Spiritual Dryness	131
63 Anger at God	133
64 Meaning of Suffering	135
65 Alienation from Religious Community	137

66 Ethical Dilemmas and Spiritual Integrity	139
67 Temptation and Spiritual Warfare	141
68 Perseverance Through Trials	143
69 Perseverance Through Persecution	145
70 Feelings of Unworthiness	147
71 Life Meaning and Purpose	149

PART V: PRAYERS FOR CONTEMPORARY STRUGGLES

72 Information Overload	153
73 Social Isolation	155
74 Pace of Life	157
75 Cyberbullying	159
76 Mental Health Awareness	161
77 Burnout	163
78 Economic Insecurity	165
79 Materialism and Consumerism	167
80 Work-Life Balance	169
81 Parenting Challenges	171
82 Single Parenting	173
83 Negative Influences	175
84 Privacy and Surveillance	177
85 Cultural Conflict	179
86 Authentic Connections	181
87 Environmental Grief	183
88 Obesity	185
89 Travel Safety	187
90 Healthcare Access	189
91 Educational Disparity	191
92 Elderly Care	193
93 Racism and Inequality	195
94 Political Division	197
95 Violence	199
96 Poverty	201
97 Homelessness	203
98 Fatherlessness	205
99 Human Trafficking	207
100 Justice	209

Part I:
Embracing Healing: Prayers for Physical Well-being

Introduction

In the journey through "Embracing Healing: Prayers for Physical Well-being," readers are invited into a sanctuary of prayers dedicated to those navigating the complexities of physical health. This collection reaches out to all who find themselves caught in the sudden clasp of illness, treading the enduring path of chronic conditions, or recovering from the scars of injury. Here, the prayers resonate with the struggle, resilience, and hope inherent in physical suffering.

More than a quest for relief, this section extends a hand of comfort, encouraging trust in a benevolent force that accompanies us in our most fragile times. It is a steadfast companion for souls searching for healing, comprehension, and the courage to persevere. These prayers remind us that in our moments of frailty, we are not isolated in our fight. They echo the promise that strength can be found even in weakness through faith, support, and divine love, illuminating our shared human experience with compassion and understanding.

01. Acute Illnesses
A Prayer for Healing and Restoration

Heavenly Father, we humbly approach Your throne of grace, seeking Your healing for those afflicted with acute illness. Your Word tells us that You mend the brokenhearted and heal their wounds. In faith, we cling to these promises, asking for Your soothing touch upon the suffering.

Lord, You declare the restoration of health and healing of wounds. Mercifully extend Your healing hands to those in need, granting relief and fortitude. Empower caregivers with wisdom and compassion, making them vessels of Your healing grace.

In Your wisdom, we submit to Your will, trusting in Your timing. Let this trial showcase Your steadfast love and might. Draw us nearer to You, fortifying our faith and reliance on Your eternal support.

Through Jesus Christ, we pray. Amen.

"He heals the brokenhearted and binds up their wounds." - Psalm 147:3

"'But I will restore you to health and heal your wounds,' declares the LORD." - Jeremiah 30:17

Prayer Notes

---

02. Chronic Conditions

A Prayer for Perseverance and Strength

---- ♥ ----

Gracious Lord, we bring before You our struggles with chronic conditions, trusting in Your promise that through Christ who strengthens us, we shall overcome. In our moments of weakness and enduring pain, let us be comforted by the sufficiency of Your eternal grace.

May Your power be perfected in our frailty, turning each day into a testimony of Your enduring strength. Grant us the patience to endure, unwavering hope, and a profound awareness of Your ever-present spirit in our journey.

Help us to look past our limitations to embrace joy and purpose. Equip us with courage for each new day, secure in the knowledge that You walk beside us. May Your unfailing strength be our solace and assurance that Your grace is sufficient, our peace.

We pray this in the powerful name of Jesus. Amen.

"I can do all this through him who gives me strength."
- Philippians 4:13
"My grace is sufficient for you, for my power is made perfect in weakness." - 2 Corinthians 12:9

Prayer Notes

03. Disability

A Prayer for Comfort and Empowerment

Heavenly Father, we lift to You, our brothers and sisters, navigating life with disabilities. Amid their challenges, let them feel Your profound love and unwavering strength, transforming perceived limitations into living testaments of Your grace.

Grant them comfort and affirm their immeasurable worth in Your eyes. Endow them with resilience that sparks joy and hope, lighting their paths. Provide a circle of support and understanding to help them surmount any obstacles.

In moments of hardship, may they and those around them find solace in Your presence. May Your power and glory shine through their lives, turning every barrier into a stepping stone for growth and inspiration.

Encourage us all to uplift one another, forging a community that cherishes each individual's contributions. In the unity of Jesus' name, we draw strength and solidarity. Amen.

"Praise be to the God and Father of our Lord Jesus Christ, the Father of compassion and the God of all comfort, who comforts us in all our troubles, so that we can comfort those in any trouble with the comfort we ourselves receive from God." - 2 Corinthians 1:3-4

Prayer Notes

_____

_____

_____

_____

_____

_____

_____

_____

_____

_____

_____

_____

_____

_____

_____

04. Injuries and Accidents
A Prayer for Healing and Divine Protection

---❤---

Heavenly Father, in the wake of injuries and unforeseen accidents, we turn to You as our healer and our unwavering source of strength. We stand on the promises of Your Word, which assures us of Your power to mend the broken and rejuvenate the weary spirits among us.

Lead us, O Lord, to be attentive to Your guiding voice, encouraging us to navigate life's uncertainties with wisdom and grace. You, the Master Healer, possess the unparalleled ability to repair the fractured, alleviate pain, and recover the lost treasures of our health and peace.

We seek Your swift healing, touching the physical and emotional wounds left in the aftermath of trials. Cloak us in Your unfailing love and instill a peace that surpasses all understanding. May this experience restore us and fortify our faith, resilience, and awareness of Your constant, nurturing presence.

In Jesus' name, we find our strength and our healing. Amen.

"He said, 'If you listen carefully to the LORD your God and do what is right in his eyes, if you pay attention to his commands and keep all his decrees, I will not bring on you any of the diseases I brought on the Egyptians, for I am the LORD, who heals you.'" - Exodus 15:26

Prayer Notes

---

05. Hormonal Imbalances
A Prayer for Balance and Well-being

---♥---

Lord, we come before You today, seeking Your healing touch on those grappling with hormonal imbalances. Inspired by John's prayer for our well-being, we ask for a health restoration that mirrors our souls' prosperity. In the areas where our bodies falter and struggle to maintain balance, we seek Your divine intervention.

Grant strength to the weary and empower the weak, as promised in Isaiah. May those affected by hormonal imbalances find their bodies responding to Your healing presence, regaining the equilibrium needed for health and vitality. Could you provide wisdom to healthcare providers to offer guidance and treatment aligned with Your will?

We pray for patience and perseverance for those on this journey so that they may experience Your peace amidst the storm. Let this time of challenge draw them closer to You, growing in faith and trust in Your loving care.

In the name of Jesus, our source of strength and healing, we pray. Amen.

"Dear friend, I pray that you may enjoy good health and that all may go well with you, even as your soul is getting along well." - 3 John 1:2

"He gives strength to the weary and increases the power of the weak." - Isaiah 40:29

Prayer Notes

_____

_____

_____

_____

_____

_____

_____

_____

_____

_____

_____

_____

_____

_____

06. Infectious Diseases

A Prayer for Recovery and Divine Safeguard

Heavenly Father, in the face of infectious diseases that threaten our well-being, we seek refuge in Your promises of sustenance and restoration. We draw comfort from Psalm 41:3, trusting in Your power to uplift those confined to their sickbeds.

We ask for Your protection over our health, as You have promised in Exodus, to shield us from harm and remove sickness from our communities. Bless our sustenance and water, and let Your healing flow through the affected areas, restoring health and igniting hope.

Empower medical professionals with the wisdom and insight needed to combat these diseases effectively. Provide comfort and peace to the afflicted and their families, surpassing all human understanding.

We trust and live in Your capable hands, in the mighty name of Jesus, our fortress and healer. Amen.

"The Lord sustains them on their sickbed and restores them from their bed of illness." - Psalm 41:3

"Worship the LORD your God, and his blessing will be on your food and water. I will take away sickness from among you." - Exodus 23:25

Prayer Notes

07. Reproductive Health Issues

A Prayer for Fertility and Blessing

---- ♥ ----

"Father in Heaven, we bring those grappling with reproductive health issues before You, finding solace in Your Word. Just as Psalm 113:9 exalts Your ability to grant the childless the joy of parenthood, we fervently pray for those yearning to welcome a child into their lives. May they experience Your gracious intervention as Hannah did, whose prayers were answered with the birth of Samuel, proclaiming with gratitude, 'I prayed for this child, and the Lord has granted me what I asked of him' (1 Samuel 1:27).

Provide them with the resilience, patience, and unwavering faith needed on their journey. Impart wisdom upon medical professionals to administer compassionate and effective care. For couples facing these challenges, fortify their relationship and deepen their trust in Your divine plan.

We entrust their hopes and dreams to Your loving will, praying for tranquility in their hearts as they await Your blessings. In Jesus' name, we ask for the precious gift of life and the incomparable joy it brings. Amen.

"He settles the childless woman in her home as a happy mother of children. Praise the Lord." - Psalm 113:9
"I prayed for this child, and the Lord has granted me what I asked of him." -1 Samuel 1:27

Prayer Notes

_____

_____

_____

_____

_____

_____

_____

_____

_____

_____

_____

_____

_____

_____

_____

08. Cancer
A Prayer for Healing and Renewal

Lord God, we approach Your throne with heavy hearts for those engaged in the battle against cancer, yet we remain anchored in hope by Your promises of healing. Echoing the faith of James 5:14-15, we seek Your anointing for the afflicted, trusting in the profound power of prayer to mend the body and elevate the spirit. May Your nurturing hand lead and comfort them, as well as their caregivers, through the arduous path ahead.

Inspire us with Paul's words in 2 Corinthians to not falter in spirit. Though our bodies may face hardship, let our inner selves be bolstered and rejuvenated each day. Illuminate our trials with the promise of the eternal glory that far outweighs our momentary challenges.

Grant those contending with cancer comfort, endurance, and a horizon filled with hope. Let them draw from Your infinite well of strength in their vulnerable moments. May Your power shine brightest in their frailty, and Your love remain steadfast through their trials.

We pray at Your feet in the healing name of Jesus, our savior and restorer. Amen.

*"Is anyone among you sick? Let them call the elders of the church to pray over them and anoint them with oil in the name of the Lord. And the prayer offered in faith will make the sick person well; the Lord will raise them up."
- James 5:14-15*

"Therefore we do not lose heart. Though outwardly we are wasting away, yet inwardly we are being renewed day by day. For our light and momentary troubles are achieving for us an eternal glory that far outweighs them all." - 2 Corinthians 4:16-18

Prayer Notes

09. Nutritional Deficiencies

A Prayer for Provision and Health

---- ♥ ----

Heavenly Father, our hearts are with those burdened by nutritional deficiencies, yet we find solace in Your word, as declared in Psalm 107:9 and Psalm 146:7—that You satisfy the thirsty and fulfill the hungry with good things. Your commitment to meeting our every need inspires hope.

We lift those deprived of essential nutrition, asking You to forge paths of provision and advocate for the marginalized. Motivate us to be Your hands and feet, sharing our abundance and understanding to eradicate hunger and malnutrition.

Empower those globally committed to resolving this plight, ensuring their endeavors are met with triumph and backing. Let every soul grappling with these challenges experience Your provision's touch, gaining the health, strength, and vitality Your boundless grace promises.

In the sustaining name of Jesus, we pray for the well-being and abundance of all. Amen.

"For he satisfies the thirsty and fills the hungry with good things." - Psalm 107:9

"He upholds the cause of the oppressed and gives food to the hungry. The Lord sets prisoners free." - Psalm 146:7

Prayer Notes

10. Inflammatory and Autoimmune Diseases
A Prayer for Grace and Strength in Weakness

--- ♥ ---

Lord God, we humbly bring before You our brothers and sisters who are enduring the daily challenges of inflammatory and autoimmune diseases. Inspired by Your word in 2 Corinthians 12:9-10, we remember Your assurance that Your grace suffices for us, and Your power reaches its full measure in our weakness.

Guide them to see their vulnerabilities as avenues for Your strength to manifest. Encourage their hearts to embrace each day with bravery, knowing that in their weakest moments, they are made strong through Your grace. Provide them the fortitude to withstand pain and uncertainty and to discover serenity and joy in Your presence amidst their trials.

We earnestly seek Your healing touch, comfort, and peace for all affected. Strengthen their faith, revealing Your omnipotence in their lives and transforming their weaknesses into a testament of Your enduring love and strength. In the compassionate and mighty name of Jesus, we pray. Amen.

"But he said to me, 'My grace is sufficient for you, for my power is made perfect in weakness.' Therefore I will boast all the more gladly about my weaknesses, so that Christ's power may rest on me. That is why, for Christ's sake, I delight in weaknesses, in insults, in hardships, in persecutions, in difficulties. For when I am weak, then I am strong." - 2 Corinthians 12:9-10

Prayer Notes

_____

_____

_____

_____

_____

_____

_____

_____

_____

_____

_____

_____

_____

_____

11. Support During Medical Treatments

A Prayer for Strength and Guidance

Heavenly Father, in the midst of medical challenges, we draw comfort from Your words in Isaiah 41:10. They remind us of Your constant presence and promise of strength, and in this assurance, we find the courage to persevere.

We seek Your wisdom for healthcare professionals guiding our treatment paths so that every decision and procedure may be under Your divine oversight. Envelop those facing treatments in Your love, granting them, along with their families, the strength and peace that surpass understanding. Let them feel Your nearness at every step, anchored in the solace of Your unwavering support.

We pray for Your blessing on the means of healing employed, trusting that You will renew health and vitality through them. Our faith rests in Your compassionate care, and we are deeply thankful for Your commitment to sustain us. In the powerful name of Jesus, we offer this prayer, seeking strength and guidance. Amen.

"So do not fear, for I am with you; do not be dismayed, for I am your God. I will strengthen you and help you; I will uphold you with my righteous right hand," - Isaiah 41:10

Prayer Notes

12 Peace in Terminal Illness
A Prayer for Comfort and Hope

Father in Heaven, amidst the journey through terminal illness, we hold tightly to the promise revealed in Revelation 21:4—that a day will come when You will tenderly wipe away every tear, and death, mourning, crying, and pain will vanish forever. For those navigating this profound challenge, we pray for an outpouring of Your peace and palpable presence.

Let them and their families find solace in the truth that the trials of our earthly existence pale in comparison to the glory of Your eternal kingdom, where joy knows no end. Bolster their hearts with the hope of what lies beyond, a future radiant with unending joy in Your presence.

Bless them with moments that reflect Your grace and the beauty of life, even in hardship. May they feel enveloped in Your love, reassured of the heavenly home that awaits. Fortify their faith to see beyond physical frailty, embracing the strength of spirit found only in Your loving embrace. In Your arms, we discover the peace to face each day and the bravery to embrace the unknown. Amen.

"He will wipe every tear from their eyes. There will be no more death or mourning or crying or pain, for the old order of things has passed away." - Revelation 21:4

Prayer Notes

13. Wisdom for Healthcare Providers

A Prayer for Dedication and Service

---- ♥ ----

Heavenly Father, we honor healthcare providers, inspired by Colossians 3:23-24 to serve as if serving You. Fill their work with Your wisdom, compassion, and grace, enabling skillful, empathetic care.

Bless their hands as extensions of Your healing, their words to comfort, and their decisions to reflect Your love. Grant them strength for demanding days and resilience against challenges, enriching their spirits with Your peace.

May their service testify to Your unfailing love, finding fulfillment in this divine calling.

In Jesus' name, we pray for their dedication and blessing. Amen.

"Whatever you do, work at it with all your heart, as working for the Lord, not for human masters, since you know that you will receive an inheritance from the Lord as a reward. It is the Lord Christ you are serving." - Colossians 3:23-24

Prayer Notes

Part II:
Nurturing the Mind: Prayers for Mental Resilience

Introduction

"Nurturing the Mind: Prayers for Mental Resilience" invites you on a journey through the intricacies of mental well-being. This section offers a compassionate embrace to those facing the shadows of anxiety, depression, and various mental health challenges. Each prayer is crafted with care to provide solace, understanding, and a pathway to inner peace and resilience.

These prayers are more than words; they are a call to strengthen the spirit, to find balance, and to rediscover hope amidst turmoil. As a companion in your journey, this collection encourages nurturing the mind with the same tenderness and dedication we afford our physical selves.

May these prayers guide you toward light and strength, reminding you of the power of faith and the comfort of divine presence in every moment of vulnerability. In this shared journey, find courage, solace, and the unshakeable belief that you are never alone.

14. Anxiety
Embracing Calm in the Storm

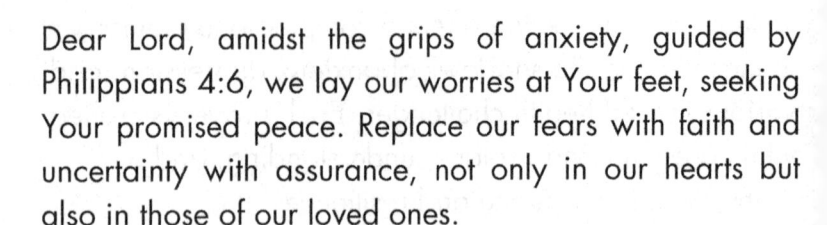

Dear Lord, amidst the grips of anxiety, guided by Philippians 4:6, we lay our worries at Your feet, seeking Your promised peace. Replace our fears with faith and uncertainty with assurance, not only in our hearts but also in those of our loved ones.

Encourage us to trust in Your providence, turning our anxious thoughts into prayers for hope. May Your peace surpass all understanding, shield our minds, calming troubled spirits. Allow this serenity to reach everyone facing anxiety, showing them Your comforting presence.

In solidarity, we resist anxiety's tide, supported by Your love. Help us bear each other's burdens, spreading Your peace in a world shadowed by worry. Amen.

"Do not be anxious about anything, but in every situation, by prayer and petition, with thanksgiving, present your requests to God." - Philippians 4:6

Prayer Notes

15. Restlessness
Finding Peace Amid Restlessness

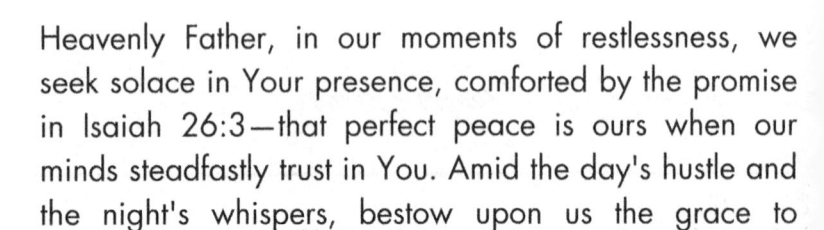

---♥---

Heavenly Father, in our moments of restlessness, we seek solace in Your presence, comforted by the promise in Isaiah 26:3—that perfect peace is ours when our minds steadfastly trust in You. Amid the day's hustle and the night's whispers, bestow upon us the grace to discover Your profound peace.

Foster in us, and in all who feel restless, a profound trust in Your divine plan. Transform our inner chaos into Your calm, reassuring us of Your unwavering care. Let this peace reside within us and extend outward, bringing tranquility to our communities in times of turmoil.

United in prayer, we pursue the deep serenity only You can offer. Guide us to anchor our hearts in Your love, spreading Your peace to every restless spirit we meet. In the name of Jesus, we pray. Amen.

"You will keep in perfect peace those whose minds are steadfast, because they trust in you." - Isaiah 26:3

Prayer Notes

---

16. Stress

Easing the Burdens of Stress

---- ♥ ----

Lord Jesus, amid life's relentless demands, we find solace in Your invitation in Matthew 11:28, calling the weary to seek refuge in You. Encircled by the burdens of stress affecting us and those around us, we look to You for relief and strength.

With Your infinite compassion, inspire us to place our worries in Your hands, trusting in Your promise to make our burdens lighter. Let Your peace refresh our tired spirits, and let this comfort reach all in search of a break from their toils, enveloping them in Your restful embrace.

May the fellowship of believers be a source of power as we support each other towards tranquility. Through our shared stories, encourage others to turn to You, finding the rest they deeply need.

In the comforting name of Jesus, our wellspring of rest and rejuvenation, we lay down our burdens and embrace Your peace. Amen.

"Come to me, all you who are weary and burdened, and I will give you rest." - Matthew 11:28

Prayer Notes

17. Fear

Bravery in the Face of Fear

Heavenly Father, amid the shadows of fear, we cling to Your word in 2 Timothy 1:7, which reminds us that You bless us not with fear but with power, love, and a sound mind. Let this truth anchor our hearts, preventing fear from finding a foothold.

Grant us, O Lord, the courage and strength to confront our fears, wrapped in Your love that drives away all dread. Lead us to a place of peace and enable us to extend that peace to those around us, shining as Your light in their darkest moments.

United in faith, may our collective courage weaken the grip of fear. Let us live out Your power and love in every challenge, embodying the bravery You inspire within us.

In Jesus' name, we choose courage over fear, anchored in Your unending presence and safeguard. Amen.

"For God has not given us a spirit of fear, but of power and of love and of a sound mind." - 2 Timothy 1:7

Prayer Notes

18. Loneliness
Finding Solace in Solitude

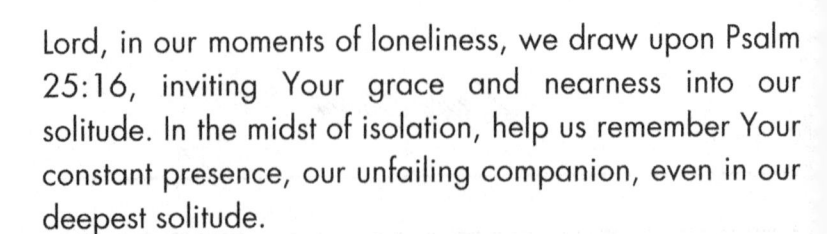

Lord, in our moments of loneliness, we draw upon Psalm 25:16, inviting Your grace and nearness into our solitude. In the midst of isolation, help us remember Your constant presence, our unfailing companion, even in our deepest solitude.

Let Your love be our comfort, turning our solitude into sacred moments of closeness with You, where we find peace and comfort in Your embrace. Move us to extend our hands to others in loneliness, spreading the warmth of Your love and the joy of community fellowship.

In the name of Jesus, who unites us in divine companionship, we seek and share Your solace and strength. Amen.

"Turn to me and be gracious to me, for I am lonely and afflicted." - Psalm 25:16

Prayer Notes

19. Depression
Paths to Healing Depression

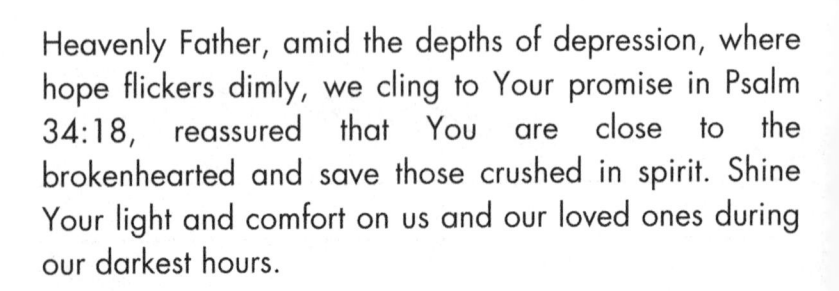

--- ♥ ---

Heavenly Father, amid the depths of depression, where hope flickers dimly, we cling to Your promise in Psalm 34:18, reassured that You are close to the brokenhearted and save those crushed in spirit. Shine Your light and comfort on us and our loved ones during our darkest hours.

Raise us from the depths of despair, enfolding us in Your comforting presence. Lead us along paths of peace and healing, allowing Your love to reach the furthest corners of our hearts. Empower us to share this profound love, providing support and empathy to others navigating their shadowed journeys.

May the Lord of all comfort envelop us in His unwavering love, guiding us from darkness into His wonderful light.

In the restorative name of Jesus, we embrace hope and begin anew. Amen.

"The LORD is close to the brokenhearted and saves those who are crushed in spirit." - Psalm 34:18

Prayer Notes

20. Despair
Light Beyond Hopelessness

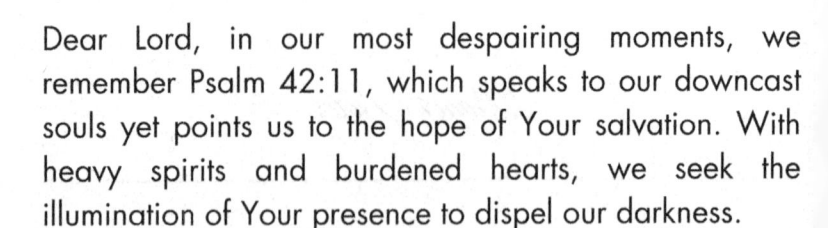

Dear Lord, in our most despairing moments, we remember Psalm 42:11, which speaks to our downcast souls yet points us to the hope of Your salvation. With heavy spirits and burdened hearts, we seek the illumination of Your presence to dispel our darkness.

As promised in Isaiah 40:31, remind us that those who hope in You will renew their strength. Instill in us the faith to soar on wings like eagles, to run without tiring, and to walk without faltering. May this hope to live within us and radiate outward, guiding and comforting those who journey through despair alongside us?

Lord of all hope, imbue us with Your peace and joy so that, empowered by the Holy Spirit, we overflow with hope, sharing Your light with everyone dwelling in despair's shadow.

In the name of Jesus, our beacon of hope, we pray. Amen.

"Why, my soul, are you downcast? Why so disturbed within me? Put your hope in God, for I will yet praise him, my Savior and my God." - Psalm 42:11

"But those who hope in the LORD will renew their strength. They will soar on wings like eagles; they will run and not grow weary, they will walk and not be faint." - Isaiah 40:31

Prayer Notes

---

21. Chronic Worry
Calming the Storms of Worry

Heavenly Father, amid the relentless waves of worry, we take comfort in the truth that our bodies are Your temples, as declared in 1 Corinthians 6:19-20. This realization comforts us, reminding us of the sacred stewardship You entrusted us—the indwelling of the Holy Spirit.

Encourage us to honor this profound gift by turning our chronic worries into prayers of surrender and trust. May we find strength in Your Spirit, peace in Your protective care, and assurance in Your unfailing love. Let our journey through worry serve as a beacon to others, showing the tranquility that comes from reliance on You.

In the name of Jesus Christ, our unshakable anchor amidst life's tempests, we pray for the serenity and bravery to embrace each day, trusting in Your everlasting care and grace. Amen.

"Do you not know that your bodies are temples of the Holy Spirit, who is in you, whom you have received from God? You are not your own; you were bought at a price. Therefore honor God with your bodies."
- 1 Corinthians 6:19-20

Prayer Notes

22. Burnout
Finding Renewal in God's Rest

---— ♥ ———

Heavenly Father, amid burnout, with our energy depleted and spirits dimming, we cling to the rest promised in Matthew 11:28-30. You call the weary to find solace in You, an offer we gratefully accept.

In our fatigue, help us to surrender our loads to You, trusting in Your nurturing care to restore us. Teach us to find balance and move in the rhythms of Your grace, recognizing that our work and rest can glorify You.

Encourage us to bear one another's burdens, reflecting Your love's light. May we discover the strength to press on, the peace to pause, and the bravery to release our stresses in Your presence.

In the name of Jesus Christ, who offers rest for our weary souls, we pray for rejuvenation, solace, and the fortitude to transcend burnout. Amen.

"Come to me, all you who are weary and burdened, and I will give you rest. Take my yoke upon you and learn from me, for I am gentle and humble in heart, and you will find rest for your souls. For my yoke is easy and my burden is light." - Matthew 11:28-30

Prayer Notes

23. Negative Self-Image
Embracing True Self-Worth

Heavenly Father, in our struggles with negative self-image, we find solace in Psalm 139:14, which affirms that we are fearfully and wonderfully made. Encourage us to accept our value as Your unique creations, crafted with purpose and care.

Help us see ourselves and one another through Your eyes of unconditional love, recognizing the intrinsic beauty and worth in every individual. May this realization empower us to uplift those battling self-doubt by sharing the truth of their immeasurable value in Your sight.

Grant us the courage to dismiss disparaging thoughts and rejoice in Your creation's diversity and splendor. Transform our hearts and minds with Your grace, nurturing a community grounded in acceptance and love.

In the name of Jesus Christ, who cherishes us beyond measure, we seek to embrace and affirm our true worth. Amen.

"I praise you because I am fearfully and wonderfully made; your works are wonderful, I know that full well."
- Psalm 139:14

Prayer Notes

---

24. Insecurity
Standing Firm in Divine Strength

Heavenly Father, when we are gripped by insecurity and doubts undermine our self-worth and direction, we draw strength from Your promise in Joshua 1:9. Reassure us of Your omnipresence, our unfailing source of comfort and guidance.

Fortify us to resist the onslaught of insecurity, to acknowledge the innate value and potential You've instilled within us. Inspire us to foster a supportive community that elevates and affirms, mirroring Your unconditional love and acceptance.

Guide us to tread confidently in the light of Your promises, fortified by Your presence and soothed by Your steadfast support. May we harness the strength and courage You impart, illuminating the world as emblems of Your radiant love.

In the unwavering love of Jesus Christ, we anchor ourselves, resilient against the currents of insecurity. Amen.

"Have I not commanded you? Be strong and courageous. Do not be afraid; do not be discouraged, for the Lord your God will be with you wherever you go." - Joshua 1:9

Prayer Notes

25. Obsessive Thoughts
Finding Peace Beyond Obsession

Lord Jesus, we seek refuge in You for clarity and tranquility during the storm of obsessive thoughts that threaten our peace. Amid our mental turmoil, bestow the serenity found only in Your presence. Guide our focus toward Your unwavering love and truth, leading our minds to a haven of peace.

Grant us the strength to entrust our persistent concerns to Your loving care. Teach us the value of trusting in Your all-encompassing control and discovering liberation in surrender. Help us extend this comfort to others facing these battles, sharing our solace in Your embrace.

May Your peace reshape our thoughts, releasing us from their relentless hold. In the mighty name of Jesus Christ, who promises that in asking, we shall receive, we plead for escape from anxiety and minds renewed in Your grace and goodness. Amen.

"We demolish arguments and every pretension that sets itself up against the knowledge of God, and we take captive every thought to make it obedient to Christ." - 2 Corinthians 10:5

Prayer Notes

---

26. Compulsions
Embracing Freedom in Christ

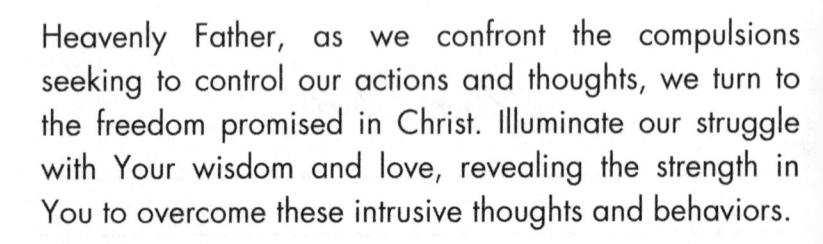

Heavenly Father, as we confront the compulsions seeking to control our actions and thoughts, we turn to the freedom promised in Christ. Illuminate our struggle with Your wisdom and love, revealing the strength in You to overcome these intrusive thoughts and behaviors.

Empower us to break free from compulsion's grasp, cultivating a deeper yearning for Your presence and peace within us. Encourage us to support each other along this journey, sharing in victories and challenges, uplifted by the knowledge of Your grace's freeing power.

In the mighty name of Jesus Christ, who proclaimed in John 8:36 that whom the Son sets free is free indeed, we pray for liberation from compulsions, the resilience to endure, and the peace that comes with living according to Your will. Grant us the courage to embrace the freedom offered through Your Son, reassured that we do not walk alone.

Amen.

"So if the Son sets you free, you will be free indeed."
- John 8:36

Prayer Notes

27. Indecisiveness
Clarity in Decision-Making

------------ ♥ ------------

Heavenly Father, as we navigate through the fog of indecision that clouds our vision, we earnestly seek the beacon of Your light to guide us. In moments filled with uncertainty, when choices loom large and clarity seems out of reach, remind us of Your unwavering presence, offering wisdom and discernment to all who come to You in faith, as promised in James 1:5.

Instill in us the courage to make decisions aligned with Your divine will, confident in the path You illuminate as righteous and fruitful. Inspire us to support each other through hesitations, collectively drawing from Your well of wisdom to light our communal journey.

In Jesus Christ's name, we pray for the gifts of clarity and decisive fortitude. May Your love touch our decisions, enabling us to proceed with peace, bolstered by the assurance of Your continuous, guiding hand.

Amen.

"If any of you lacks wisdom, you should ask God, who gives generously to all without finding fault, and it will be given to you." - James 1:5

Prayer Notes

28. Confusion

Finding God's Direction in the Midst of Uncertainty

---♥---

Lord, in the swirling mists of confusion that cloud our lives, we reach out for Your hand. With paths obscured and hearts heavy with uncertainty, we rely on Your eternal wisdom, trusting You to illuminate our way as promised in 1 Corinthians 14:33, for You are not a God of confusion but of peace.

Grant us the Holy Spirit's discernment to navigate this fog and recognize Your voice among many. Encourage us to support and guide each other, building a community of faith marked by unity and clarity.

In the name of Jesus Christ, we beseech You to dispel confusion and grant us clear minds and the tranquility that emerges from Your guiding light. Confident in Your truth and comforted by Your constant presence, may we proceed with assurance in every decision. Amen.

"For God is not a God of confusion but of peace." - 1 Corinthians 14:33

Prayer Notes

29. Mental Blocks
Unlocking Creativity and Flow

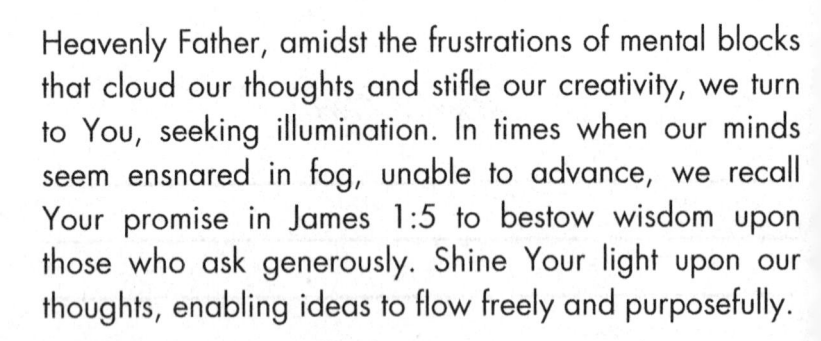

Heavenly Father, amidst the frustrations of mental blocks that cloud our thoughts and stifle our creativity, we turn to You, seeking illumination. In times when our minds seem ensnared in fog, unable to advance, we recall Your promise in James 1:5 to bestow wisdom upon those who ask generously. Shine Your light upon our thoughts, enabling ideas to flow freely and purposefully.

Empower us with the resilience to navigate past these barriers, firm in the belief that through Your guidance, no obstacle is insurmountable. Inspire us to uplift one another, exchanging insights and bolstering spirits as we pursue a clear vision and creativity together.

In the name of Jesus, our wellspring of wisdom and might, we petition for the dissolution of mental blocks and the liberation of our creativity, all under Your sovereign direction. Amen.

"If any of you lacks wisdom, you should ask God, who gives generously to all without finding fault, and it will be given to you." - James 1:5

Prayer Notes

---

30. Self-Harm
Seeking Healing and Wholeness

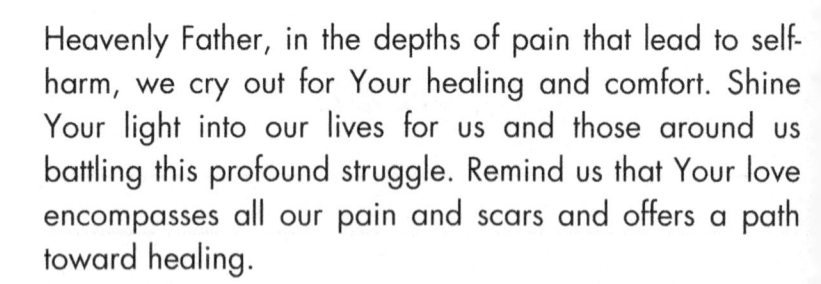

Heavenly Father, in the depths of pain that lead to self-harm, we cry out for Your healing and comfort. Shine Your light into our lives for us and those around us battling this profound struggle. Remind us that Your love encompasses all our pain and scars and offers a path toward healing.

Empower us with the strength to resist harming ourselves and to seek the help we need. Provide us with a supportive community that understands, cares, and walks alongside us in our journey towards recovery. Help us to remember that our bodies are temples of the Holy Spirit, deserving of care and respect.

In the name of Jesus, our healer and redeemer, we pray for freedom from the urge to harm ourselves. Grant us peace, healing, and the assurance of Your unfailing love. Amen.

"Do you not know that your bodies are temples of the Holy Spirit, who is in you, whom you have received from God? You are not your own; you were bought at a price. Therefore honor God with your bodies." - 1 Corinthians 6:19-20

Prayer Notes

31. Suicidal Thoughts
Embracing Hope in Despair

--- ♥ ---

Lord, amidst the darkest thoughts that cloud our minds, where hope seems extinguished and the will to continue fades, we seek Your light and life. For anyone among us grappling with the shadow of suicidal thoughts, we pray for Your intervention, Your comfort, and Your peace. Let them feel Your presence, a beacon of hope in their darkest night.

Grant us, O God, the wisdom to recognize the cries for help, the courage to reach out with love and understanding, and the strength to support those in their most vulnerable moments. Instill a spirit of compassion and empathy to be there for one another, reminding each soul of their invaluable worth in Your eyes.

In the name of Jesus, our refuge and our hope, we pray for all who battle with thoughts of ending their lives. Surround them with Your love, lead them from despair to hope, and remind them that there is always a reason to live with You. Amen.

"The Lord is close to the brokenhearted and saves those who are crushed in spirit." - Psalm 34:18

Prayer Notes

32. Addiction
Finding Strength in Liberation

Heavenly Father, in the grip of addiction, where freedom seems beyond our reach, and the battle tires our souls, we call upon Your strength and mercy. For ourselves and for those we know struggling under the weight of addiction, we pray for Your guiding light to lead us out of the darkness.

Empower us with Your Holy Spirit to face this challenge with courage and determination. Grant us the clarity to see the path of recovery, the will to walk it, and the perseverance to sustain it. Help us to build a supportive community that offers understanding, encouragement, and accountability in moments of weakness.

In the name of Jesus, our Deliverer, we seek Your healing and liberation from the chains of addiction. May we find renewal in Your grace, embracing the freedom and life You offer with open hearts. Amen.

"So if the Son sets you free, you will be free indeed."
- John 8:36

Prayer Notes

33. Eating Disorders
Nourishing Body and Soul

Heavenly Father, amidst the struggles with eating disorders that torment our bodies and spirits, we seek Your compassionate embrace. For those battling to find balance and health, illuminate our path with Your love and wisdom. Remind us of our worth in Your eyes, beyond physical appearances or societal measures.

Grant us the strength to confront the underlying pains and fears fueling these disorders. Provide us with a circle of support—family, friends, and professionals—who understand, encourage, and guide us toward healing. Help us to cherish our bodies as temples of the Holy Spirit, deserving of care and respect.

In the name of Jesus, our Healer, we pray for recovery and peace for all suffering from eating disorders. Lead us to a place of acceptance and self-love, where we nourish our bodies as an act of gratitude for Your precious gift of life. Amen.

"Do you not know that your bodies are temples of the Holy Spirit, who is in you, whom you have received from God? You are not your own; you were bought at a price. Therefore honor God with your bodies." - 1 Corinthians 6:19-20

Prayer Notes

34. Insomnia and Sleep Disorder
Restful Nights, Peaceful Minds

---- ♥ ----

Heavenly Father, in the stillness of the night, when sleep eludes us, and restlessness takes hold, we turn to You, seeking the peace that surpasses all understanding. For ourselves and for those among us wrestling with insomnia and sleep disorders, we ask for Your comforting presence to envelop us, easing our minds and calming our spirits.

Grant us the gift of restful sleep, a renewal for our bodies and souls. May we awaken refreshed and rejuvenated, ready to embrace the day with joy and gratitude? Help us establish patterns and environments that promote healthy sleep, trusting in Your design for our well-being.

In the name of Jesus, our source of rest and renewal, we pray to alleviate insomnia and sleep disorders. May we find solace in Your promise of rest for the weary, laying down our burdens and fears at Your feet and waking to the light of Your new day? Amen.

"In peace I will lie down and sleep, for you alone, Lord, make me dwell in safety." - Psalm 4:8

Prayer Notes

35. Trauma
Healing from Trauma and Renewal

Heavenly Father, in the aftermath of trauma, where memories linger and shadows of the past loom large, we seek Your healing and peace. For all of us touched by traumatic experiences, grant us the courage to face our pain, the strength to heal, and the faith to move forward.

Surround us with Your love and grace, offering comfort in moments of distress and hope in times of despair. Provide us with a supportive community that understands, empathizes, and aids in our journey toward recovery. Help us to trust in Your ability to restore our brokenness and to find beauty in our scars.

In the name of Jesus, our Healer, and Protector, we pray for deep healing from trauma, renewed spirits, and the peace that comes from laying our burdens at Your feet. May we emerge from this valley with a stronger faith and a testimony of Your unfailing love. Amen.

"He heals the brokenhearted and binds up their wounds." - Psalm 147:3

Prayer Notes

36. Post-Traumatic Stress Disorder (PTSD)

Seeking Peace in the Aftermath

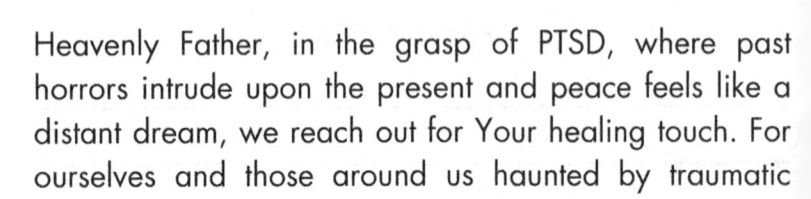

Heavenly Father, in the grasp of PTSD, where past horrors intrude upon the present and peace feels like a distant dream, we reach out for Your healing touch. For ourselves and those around us haunted by traumatic memories, we ask for Your comforting presence to envelop us, dispelling the darkness with Your light.

Grant us strength to confront our fears, resilience to endure our healing journey, and hope to envision a life beyond the pain. Provide us with compassionate souls to walk alongside us, offering understanding, support, and love as we navigate the challenging path to recovery.

In the name of Jesus, our Refuge and Strength, we pray for relief from the symptoms of PTSD, for the restoration of peace in our minds, and the renewal of joy in our hearts. May we find solace in Your promise of a future where fear is replaced by faith and turmoil by tranquility? Amen.

"Peace I leave with you; my peace I give you. I do not give to you as the world gives. Do not let your hearts be troubled and do not be afraid." - John 14:27

Prayer Notes

37. Attention Deficit Hyperactivity Disorder (PTSD)
Harnessing Focus and Energy

Father in Heaven, we come before You today, humbly asking for Your guidance and strength for those among us struggling with ADHD. Help them find focus amidst the chaos, and grant them peace in their hearts and minds. Let Your love and patience guide them, offering solace and understanding in their moments of confusion and frustration.

Empower them, O Lord, with the perseverance to overcome obstacles and the wisdom to recognize their unique gifts. Surround them with a community of support that nurtures and accepts them, reflecting Your endless love. Provide them and those who walk alongside them with the strength to advocate for their needs and the grace to accept themselves as beautifully made in Your image.

In the name of Jesus Christ, we pray for those touched by ADHD so that they may embrace their journey with faith and courage, knowing You are with them every step of the way. Amen.

"My grace is sufficient for you, for my power is made perfect in weakness." - 2 Corinthians 12:9

Prayer Notes

38. Obsessive-Compulsive Disorder(OCD)

Managing OCD with Grace

Heavenly Father, in the stillness of our hearts, we come before You seeking Your grace and strength. For those among us wrestling with the trials of OCD, grant them Your peace that surpasses understanding. Help them navigate their days with faith and resilience, trusting in Your unfailing love.

Lord, guide us to be a source of support and understanding for those affected. Teach us to listen with compassion, respond with kindness, and walk beside them in their journey towards healing. May Your wisdom enlighten their paths and Your grace soothe their anxieties.

In all things, we pray for Your will to be done, for strength in moments of weakness, and for the courage to embrace each day with hope. Remember that we are never alone in our struggles, for You are with us, carrying our burdens and transforming our trials into triumphs. Through Your mercy, may we manage OCD with grace and find solace in Your eternal love. Amen.

"Do not be anxious about anything, but in every situation, by prayer and petition, with thanksgiving, present your requests to God. And the peace of God, which transcends all understanding, will guard your hearts and your minds in Christ Jesus." - Philippians 4:6-7

Prayer Notes

39. Schizophrenia

Understanding and Supporting Schizophrenia

Lord, we lift those touched by the veil of schizophrenia, seeking Your light in their moments of darkness. Grant them courage and strength, and infuse their hearts with Your unending peace. May Your presence be a beacon of hope, guiding them through the complexities of their journey.

Bless the caregivers with patience and understanding, fortifying them with love and wisdom to be pillars of support. Encourage the medical professionals and therapists who provide care so that their efforts may be guided by Your hand, bringing healing and comfort.

In Your grace, provide moments of clarity and joy amidst the challenges. Strengthen the bonds of community and family around those affected so that they may feel not isolation but the warmth of Your love through the support of others. May trust in Your providence lead us all toward compassion, acceptance, and the pursuit of holistic well-being. Amen.

"Casting all your anxieties on Him, because He cares for you." - 1 Peter 5:7

Prayer Notes

40. Bipolar Disorder
Balancing Life with Bipolar Disorder

Heavenly Father, we seek Your guidance and comfort for those living with bipolar disorder. Grant them strength and steadiness amidst the ebbs and flows of their emotions. Provide them a sense of balance that only Your grace can offer, illuminating their paths with hope and clarity.

Encourage us to be compassionate allies, offering support and understanding. Let our actions and words reflect Your love, helping to build a community of care and acceptance around them.

In their moments of darkness and their moments of light, remind them that they are never alone, for You are with them, offering peace that surpasses all understanding.

In the name of Jesus, our Savior, We pray, Amen.

"And the peace of God, which transcends all understanding, will guard your hearts and your minds in Christ Jesus." - Philippians 4:7

Prayer Notes

41. Psychotic Disorders
Navigating the World of Psychotic Disorders

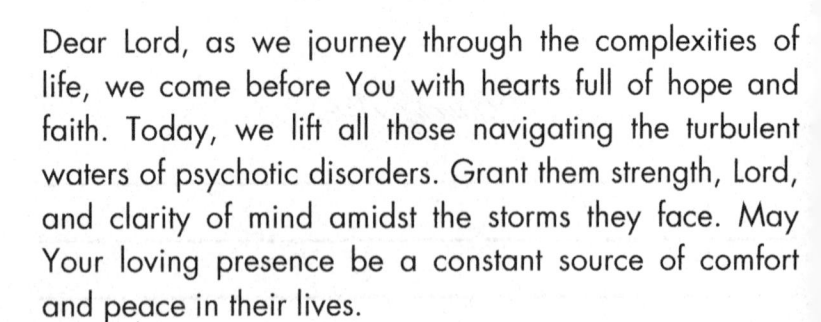

Dear Lord, as we journey through the complexities of life, we come before You with hearts full of hope and faith. Today, we lift all those navigating the turbulent waters of psychotic disorders. Grant them strength, Lord, and clarity of mind amidst the storms they face. May Your loving presence be a constant source of comfort and peace in their lives.

We pray for the families and friends who stand by their loved ones during these challenging times. Provide them with patience, understanding, and unwavering support. Help them to be anchors of love and sources of encouragement, reflecting Your boundless compassion and care.

As we seek guidance and healing, we ask for wisdom from the professionals dedicated to helping those affected by psychotic disorders. May their knowledge and expertise be tools used for restoration, guided by Your hand. In the name of Jesus, our Supreme Guide, we pray for their unwavering commitment and divine favor. Amen.

"For God has not given us a spirit of fear, but of power and of love and of a sound mind." - 2 Timothy 1:7

Prayer Notes

---

42. Personality Disorders
Compassionate Understanding of Personality Disorders

Heavenly Father, we seek Your guidance and comfort in Your infinite wisdom and mercy. For those among us journeying through the complexities of personality disorders, we ask for Your enveloping love to surround them. Grant them resilience, understanding, and the courage to face their daily challenges with hope and dignity.

We pray for their families, friends, and caregivers that they may offer unwavering support, empathy, and kindness. May their actions be guided by Your example of unconditional love, helping to forge paths of understanding and acceptance in their relationships.

Bestow wisdom, patience, and strength upon the professionals and advocates working tirelessly in this field. May Your grace illuminate their efforts, leading to breakthroughs and healing. In the name of Jesus, our Compassionate Savior, we pray for their relentless pursuit of care and healing. Amen.

"Therefore, as God's chosen people, holy and dearly loved, clothe yourselves with compassion, kindness, humility, gentleness and patience." - Colossians 3:12

Prayer Notes

43. Cognitive Disorders
Supporting Minds with Cognitive Disorders

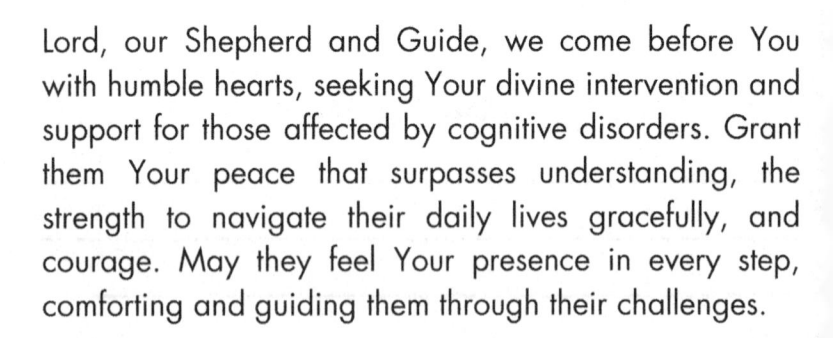

Lord, our Shepherd and Guide, we come before You with humble hearts, seeking Your divine intervention and support for those affected by cognitive disorders. Grant them Your peace that surpasses understanding, the strength to navigate their daily lives gracefully, and courage. May they feel Your presence in every step, comforting and guiding them through their challenges.

We lift the caregivers, families, and friends of those with cognitive disorders, asking for Your wisdom and patience to fill their hearts. Empower them with empathy and resilience, enabling them to provide the necessary support and love, reflecting Your infinite care and compassion.

For the healthcare professionals and researchers dedicated to understanding and treating cognitive disorders, we pray for insight and breakthroughs under Your guidance. May their work be blessed with progress and hope for those they serve. In the name of Jesus, our Ultimate Healer, we pray for their steadfast commitment and Your continued blessings upon them. Amen.

"Cast all your anxiety on Him because He cares for you." - *1 Peter 5:7*

Prayer Notes

44. Neurodevelopmental Disorders
Empathy for Neurodevelopmental Challenges

Loving Father, in Your vast creation, each of us is wonderfully made, yet some of Your children face unique challenges in their neurodevelopmental journeys. We pray that those experiencing neurodevelopmental disorders may find strength in Your love and confidence in their value. Illuminate their paths with hope, understanding, and the joy of Your constant presence.

We also pray for the families, educators, and therapists who walk alongside them. Equip these companions with empathy, patience, and wisdom to offer support and encouragement. May they be mirrors of Your love, helping to highlight each individual's strengths and abilities.

For the community and society, inspire us to create inclusive environments where everyone is respected and valued for their uniqueness. In the name of Jesus, our Protector and Guide, we pray for unity, dedication, and blessings upon all who are touched by neurodevelopmental disorders. Amen.

"For you created my inmost being; you knit me together in my mother's womb. I praise you because I am fearfully and wonderfully made; your works are wonderful, I know that full well." - Psalm 139:13-14

Prayer Notes

45. Self-Doubt and Imposter Syndrome

Subduing the Shadows

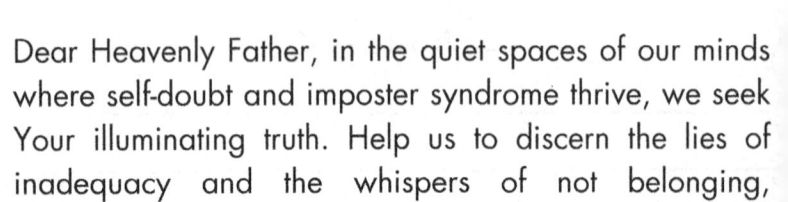

Dear Heavenly Father, in the quiet spaces of our minds where self-doubt and imposter syndrome thrive, we seek Your illuminating truth. Help us to discern the lies of inadequacy and the whispers of not belonging, replacing them with Your affirmations of worth and belonging. Fortify our hearts with Your courage and our minds with Your peace, enabling us to stand firm in our identities as Your beloved children.

We pray for those around us wrestling with these same shadows. May we be vessels of Your love, encouraging one another with words of truth and acts of kindness. Let our community be a haven of acceptance, where every person is valued for their true self, free from the weight of doubt and the mask of pretense.

For all who lead, teach, and influence, grant them the wisdom to nurture confidence and authenticity in those they guide. In the name of Jesus, our Anchor and Light, we pray. Amen.

"Be strong and courageous. Do not be afraid or terrified because of them, for the Lord your God goes with you; He will never leave you nor forsake you." - Deuteronomy 31:6

Prayer Notes

46. Body Dysmorphia
Seeing Beauty Within

Heavenly Father, in a world obsessed with external appearances, we seek Your grace to recognize the true beauty within us. For those struggling with body dysmorphia, we ask for Your healing touch on their hearts and minds. Illuminate their perspective with Your love, allowing them to see themselves as You see them—beautiful, unique, and wonderfully made.

Grant them the strength to combat negative thoughts and the courage to embrace their individuality. May Your unconditional love be a balm to their souls, reminding them of their worth beyond physical appearances.

We pray for a supportive community that uplifts and affirms the value of every person, not for what they look like, but for who they are in Your eyes. In the name of Jesus, our Source of True Beauty, we pray for their liberation from these chains and Your everlasting peace and acceptance. Amen.

"I praise you, for I am fearfully and wonderfully made. Wonderful are your works; my soul knows it very well."
- Psalm 139:14

Prayer Notes

Part III:
Nurturing the Heart: Prayers for Emotional Wellness

Introduction

"Nurturing the Heart: Prayers for Emotional Wellness" ushers you into a profound exploration of emotional health, guiding you through the complexities of the human heart with divine comfort and strength. This collection journeys into the spectrum of emotions—from disappointment's sting and rejection's ache to insecurity's challenge and sorrow's depth. Each prayer, a heartfelt dialogue with the Divine, offers solace amid change, uncertainty, fears, and the enigmatic unknown.

Together, we address self-esteem hurdles, jealousy, envy's sharp edges, and the tangles of relationship woes. We tread through guilt and shame's shadows, anger and resentment, betrayal, the anxiety of death, and the intense landscape of grief and loss. Crafted to uplift, heal, and strengthen, these prayers assure us of our never-alone stance in facing emotional battles.

47. Disappointment
Navigating Through Letdowns

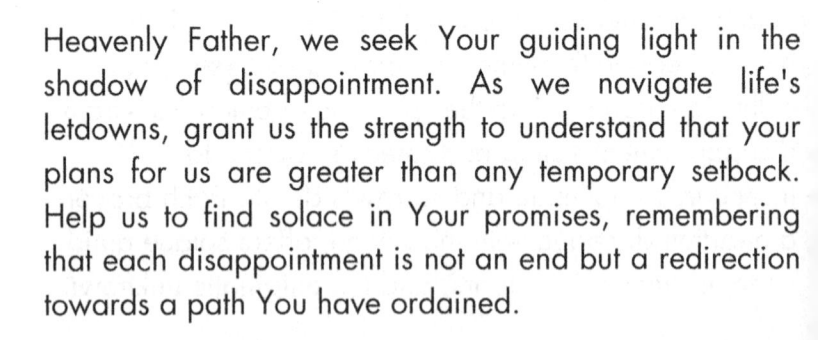

Heavenly Father, we seek Your guiding light in the shadow of disappointment. As we navigate life's letdowns, grant us the strength to understand that your plans for us are greater than any temporary setback. Help us to find solace in Your promises, remembering that each disappointment is not an end but a redirection towards a path You have ordained.

In this journey, we ask for the grace to remain patient and steadfast, trusting in Your timing and wisdom. May we view our disappointments not as failures but as opportunities for growth and deeper faith. Let this understanding fill our hearts with peace and resilience.

We pray for all those experiencing the sting of unmet expectations that they may find comfort and guidance in Your loving embrace.

In the name of Jesus, our Steadfast Hope, we pray for their continued dedication and blessing. Amen.

"And we know that in all things God works for the good of those who love him, who have been called according to his purpose." - Romans 8:28

Prayer Notes

48. Rejection
Finding Strength in Refusal

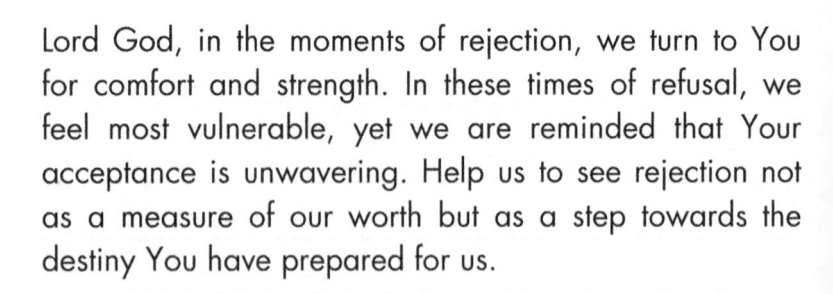

---❤---

Lord God, in the moments of rejection, we turn to You for comfort and strength. In these times of refusal, we feel most vulnerable, yet we are reminded that Your acceptance is unwavering. Help us to see rejection not as a measure of our worth but as a step towards the destiny You have prepared for us.

Grant us the courage to face rejection with grace, using it as a catalyst for growth and self-reflection. May we lean into Your love, finding solace and strength in Your embrace. Teach us to use these experiences to deepen our compassion and empathy for others, becoming beacons of Your unconditional love.

We pray that all those grappling with the pain of rejection may find resilience in their hearts and continue forward.

In the name of Jesus, our Refuge and Strength, we pray for their continued dedication and blessing. Amen.

"The stone the builders rejected has become the cornerstone;" - Psalm 118:22

Prayer Notes

---

49. Insecurities
Cultivating Confidence Within

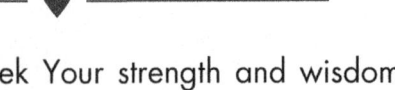

Almighty Father, we seek Your strength and wisdom in the quiet battles with our insecurities. In moments of doubt, remind us of the unshakeable worth You have placed within us. Guide us to see ourselves through Your eyes: cherished, capable, and made with purpose. Help us to cultivate a deep-rooted confidence that stands firm against the storms of self-doubt.

Empower us, Lord, to use our insecurities as stepping stones towards growth, not as barriers to our potential. May Your love be the mirror in which we view ourselves, transforming our insecurities into opportunities for affirmation and self-discovery. Teach us to extend grace to ourselves, embracing our flaws and strengths as You do.

We pray for Your enveloping peace and reassurance for all who struggle with inadequacy. We pray for their continued dedication and blessing in the name of Jesus, our Source of Confidence. Amen.

"for God gave us a spirit not of fear but of power and love and self-control." - 2 Timothy 1:7

Prayer Notes

50. Sorrow

Seeking Solace in Sadness

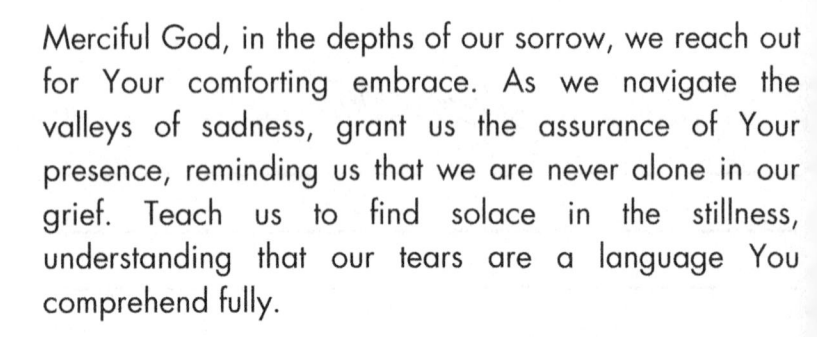

♥

Merciful God, in the depths of our sorrow, we reach out for Your comforting embrace. As we navigate the valleys of sadness, grant us the assurance of Your presence, reminding us that we are never alone in our grief. Teach us to find solace in the stillness, understanding that our tears are a language You comprehend fully.

Encourage our hearts, O Lord, to seek Your peace, which transcends all understanding. May this peace guard our hearts and minds, offering a refuge in the midst of our sorrow. Help us grasp the lessons woven within our pain, finding hope and strength in Your enduring love.

We lift all those burdened with sadness, praying for the light of Your comfort to pierce their darkness. In the name of Jesus, our Comforter, in times of distress, we pray for their continued dedication and blessing. Amen.

"Blessed are those who mourn, for they shall be comforted." - Matthew 5:4

Prayer Notes

51. Change and Uncertainty
Embracing the Unpredictable

Lord of all seasons, in the midst of change and uncertainty, we seek Your guiding light. Teach us to embrace the unpredictable journey of life with a heart of trust and surrender. Remind us that though the path may twist and turn, Your steadfast love remains our constant and sure foundation.

Grant us the grace to let go of our need for control and the courage to step into the unknown in Your providential care confidently. Help us to see each change not as a threat but as an opportunity for growth and new blessings. Strengthen our faith to navigate these times, finding peace in the promise of Your presence every step of the way.

For all those facing the anxieties of transitions, may they find solace in the assurance of Your unchanging nature.

In the name of Jesus, our Anchor in every storm, we pray for their continued dedication and blessing. Amen.

"Trust in the Lord with all your heart, and do not lean on your own understanding. In all your ways acknowledge Him, and He will make straight your paths." - Proverbs 3:5-6

Prayer Notes

52. Fears, Phobias, and the Unknown

Overcoming Anxiety's Grip

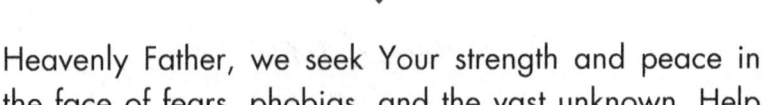

Heavenly Father, we seek Your strength and peace in the face of fears, phobias, and the vast unknown. Help us to remember that You are bigger than our biggest fears and that Your perfect love casts out all anxiety. Grant us the courage to confront what frightens us, not alone but with the assurance of Your presence beside us.

Teach us to breathe in Your peace in moments of panic and to walk in faith through the shadows of uncertainty. Let Your Word be the lamp unto our feet, guiding us through dark places with the light of Your wisdom and truth.

We pray for all those entangled in the grip of anxiety that they may experience Your liberating love.

In the name of Jesus, our Protector, and Peace, we pray for their continued dedication and blessing. Amen.

"Peace I leave with you; my peace I give to you. Not as the world gives do I give to you. Let not your hearts be troubled, neither let them be afraid." - John 14:27

Prayer Notes

53. Self-Esteem Challenges
Building Self-Worth Step by Step

Gracious God, who created us in Your image and likeness, we come before You with hearts seeking to overcome self-esteem challenges. In moments of doubt and self-criticism, remind us of our inherent worth in Your eyes. Help us to see the beauty and value You have instilled in us, guiding us to build our self-worth upon the foundation of Your unconditional love.

Empower us, Lord, to take each step towards positive self-regard with the confidence that comes from knowing we are Your beloved. Teach us to replace negative thoughts with affirmations of our identity as Your children, capable and loved. May we grow in the understanding that external validations do not determine our worth but by Your eternal love for us.

We pray for Your encouragement and strength for all those wrestling with feelings of inadequacy. We pray for their continued dedication and blessing in the name of Jesus, our Firm Foundation. Amen.

"I praise you because I am fearfully and wonderfully made; your works are wonderful, I know that full well."
- Psalm 139:14

Prayer Notes

54. Jealousy and Envy
Transforming Envy into Empowerment

---♥---

Lord of all grace, we seek Your wisdom and transformation in feelings of jealousy and envy. Help us to understand the root of our envy and guide us to channel these feelings into motivations for our growth and betterment. Teach us to celebrate the successes of others as we remember that Your blessings are abundant and unique to each of our journeys.

Encourage us, O God, to focus on the talents and gifts You have bestowed upon us. Empower us to use our abilities for Your glory, finding contentment in our path. May the energy spent on envy be redirected towards cultivating gratitude for what we have and who we are in You.

We pray that all those struggling with jealousy may find liberation in Your love and strength in their individuality.

In the name of Jesus, our Source of Self-Worth, we pray for their continued dedication and blessing. Amen.

"Let us not become conceited, provoking one another, envying one another." - Galatians 5:26

Prayer Notes

55. Relationship Pains
Healing Hearts Together

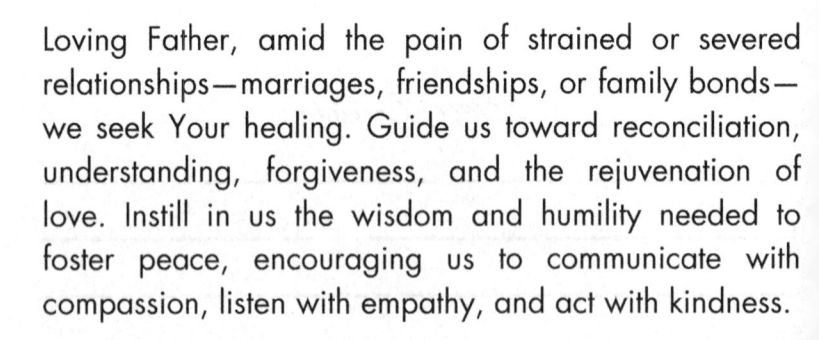

--- ♥ ---

Loving Father, amid the pain of strained or severed relationships—marriages, friendships, or family bonds—we seek Your healing. Guide us toward reconciliation, understanding, forgiveness, and the rejuvenation of love. Instill in us the wisdom and humility needed to foster peace, encouraging us to communicate with compassion, listen with empathy, and act with kindness.

By Your grace, empower us to forgive and love unconditionally, making our interactions reflect Your profound love. Transform our relationships into bastions of mutual support, growth, and joy.

In Jesus' name, we ask for healing for ourselves and comfort for all facing relational challenges, trusting in Your promise of unity, understanding, and the renewal of bonds. Amen.

"Bear with each other and forgive one another if any of you has a grievance against someone. Forgive as the Lord forgave you." - Colossians 3:13

Prayer Notes

56. Guilt and Shame
Liberating the Self from Regret

Merciful God, as we navigate the deep waters of guilt and shame, we seek Your light for liberation and redemption. Enlighten us with Your forgiveness, teaching us that our past does not confine our worth. Help us embrace Your grace, releasing the chains of regret and self-condemnation.

Lead us on a healing path to forgive ourselves as You graciously forgive us. Let us grow from our missteps without being ensnared by them, stepping forward with hope and a renewed heart. May Your enduring love remind us that we transcend our lowest points, bathed in Your mercy each new day.

We pray for reassurance and peace for everyone wrestling with guilt and shame.

In the name of Jesus, our Hope and Redeemer, we ask for strength and grace to overcome and the blessing of renewed dedication in our lives and communities. Amen.

"Therefore, there is now no condemnation for those who are in Christ Jesus." - Romans 8:1

Prayer Notes

57. Betrayal
Rebuilding Trust from Ashes

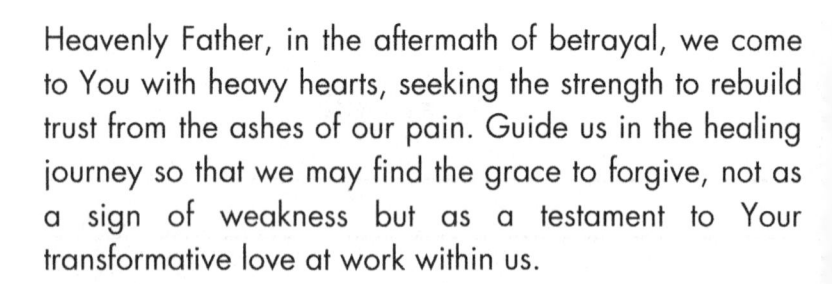

Heavenly Father, in the aftermath of betrayal, we come to You with heavy hearts, seeking the strength to rebuild trust from the ashes of our pain. Guide us in the healing journey so that we may find the grace to forgive, not as a sign of weakness but as a testament to Your transformative love at work within us.

Help us discern the pathways of reconciliation where possible and grant us the wisdom to establish healthy boundaries where necessary. Infuse our spirits with Your peace so that we may overcome bitterness and move forward with hope and resilience. Teach us to trust again, beginning with our trust in You, knowing that You are faithful even when others are not.

For all who have been wounded by betrayal, we pray for Your comforting presence and healing touch. We pray for their continued dedication and blessing in the name of Jesus, our Solid Rock. Amen.

"Do not be overcome by evil, but overcome evil with good." - Romans 12:21

Prayer Notes

58. Anger and Resentment
Releasing Bitterness for Peace

Holy and Just God, amidst the flames of anger and the weight of resentment, we seek Your cooling waters of peace. Teach us to release our grip on bitterness, that it may not poison our hearts but rather be transformed into a bridge to understanding and reconciliation. Help us to see beyond our hurt, recognizing the humanity in those who have wronged us.

Grant us the strength to forgive, not because it absolves wrongdoing, but because it frees our hearts to experience Your peace. Remind us that holding onto anger binds us more than those at whom it is directed. Instill in us a spirit of humility and patience to approach conflicts with a heart-seeking resolution and unity.

For everyone entangled in the snares of anger and resentment, we ask for Your guidance towards paths of healing and peace. We pray for their continued dedication and blessing in the name of Jesus, our Prince of Peace. Amen.

"Let all bitterness and wrath and anger and clamor and slander be put away from you, along with all malice. Be kind to one another, tenderhearted, forgiving one another, as God in Christ forgave you." - Ephesians 4:31-32

Prayer Notes

59. Death Anxiety
Facing Mortality with Courage

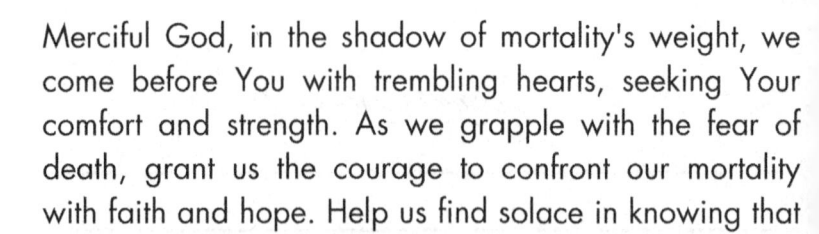

Merciful God, in the shadow of mortality's weight, we come before You with trembling hearts, seeking Your comfort and strength. As we grapple with the fear of death, grant us the courage to confront our mortality with faith and hope. Help us find solace in knowing that You are the Author of life and the Keeper of eternity.

Teach us to live each day with purpose and gratitude, cherishing the gift of life You have entrusted to us. May our fear of death be transformed into a reverence for the sanctity of life and a readiness to meet You when our time on earth is complete.

We pray for all who are plagued by death anxiety that they may find peace in the assurance of Your presence and the promise of eternal life. We pray for their continued dedication and blessing in the name of Jesus, our Everlasting Hope. Amen.

"Even though I walk through the valley of the shadow of death, I will fear no evil, for you are with me; your rod and your staff, they comfort me." - Psalm 23:4

Prayer Notes

60. Grief and Loss
Embracing Calm in the Storm

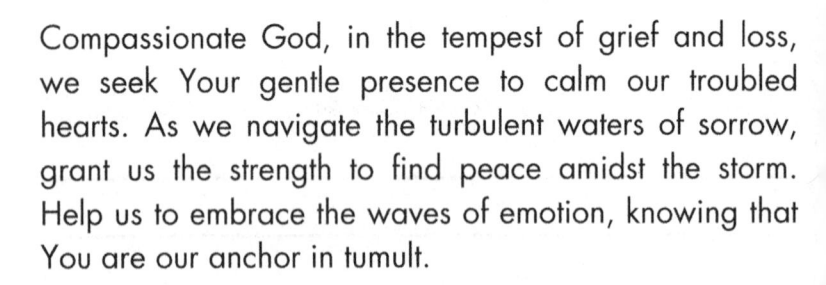

Compassionate God, in the tempest of grief and loss, we seek Your gentle presence to calm our troubled hearts. As we navigate the turbulent waters of sorrow, grant us the strength to find peace amidst the storm. Help us to embrace the waves of emotion, knowing that You are our anchor in tumult.

Teach us to cherish the memories of those we have lost, finding comfort in the love we shared. May we draw closer to You in our grief, trusting in Your promise of comfort and restoration. Guide us to lean on one another for support, sharing our burdens as we journey through the valley of loss.

We lift all who mourn the absence of loved ones, asking for Your tender mercy to soothe their pain and heal their souls. In the name of Jesus, our Comforter, in times of sorrow, we pray for their continued dedication and blessing. Amen.

"Blessed are those who mourn, for they shall be comforted." - Matthew 5:4

Prayer Notes

Part IV:
Nurturing the Mind: Prayers for Spiritual Crises

Introduction

In "Nurturing the Mind: Prayers for Spiritual Crises," this part of the prayer book walks you through the spiritual uncertainty fog. It's for moments when faith flickers low, and doubts rise high when God feels distant, and your heart feels empty. It's for times when anger at the divine simmers within, and suffering seems senseless. It's for those who feel cut off from their spiritual family, face tough choices that tug at their conscience, and find themselves wrestling with temptations that threaten their peace.

These prayers are companions for the journey through hard days, offering words for when your own are hard to find. They're about holding on when everything seems to push you to let go, finding worth in yourself when you feel overlooked, and searching for a bigger picture when life feels painfully tiny. Here, you'll find prayers that understand, give voice to the struggle, and reach for hope when all seems lost. They're about getting through the dark times together, one step at a time.

61. Doubt and Unbelief
Embracing Faithfulness

---- ♥ ----

Gracious God, we come before You in moments of inner turmoil, where doubt clouds the firmament of our souls. In the stillness of our hearts, we seek the light of Your unwavering truth to guide us back to a place of trust.

For every trembling spirit and wavering heart, we ask for the grace to overcome the seas of uncertainty. May we find strength in the testament of Your works and the whispers of Your assurances that resonate within the scriptures and the echoes of our faith community.

In the name of Jesus, our Great Anchor, we pray for steadfastness and rejuvenation of belief in our journey toward a faith that does not falter. May Your wisdom be the compass that leads us from the shadows of doubt into the dawn of unfaltering trust. Amen.

"But when you ask, you must believe and not doubt, because the one who doubts is like a wave of the sea, blown and tossed by the wind." - James 1:6
"I believe; help my unbelief!" - Mark 9:24

Prayer Notes

62. Distant from God/Spiritual Dryness

Cultivating Spiritual Presence

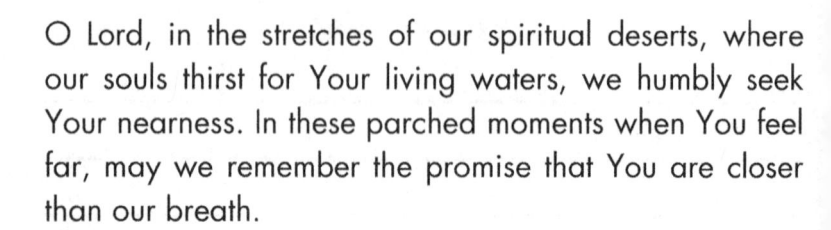

O Lord, in the stretches of our spiritual deserts, where our souls thirst for Your living waters, we humbly seek Your nearness. In these parched moments when You feel far, may we remember the promise that You are closer than our breath.

For ourselves and all who wander in the barren lands of faith, longing for a sign of Your presence, we ask for the dew of Your Spirit to quench our dryness. Let the soft rains of Your grace revive and replenish the arid places within us.

In the name of Jesus, our Fountain of Hope, we pray to revitalize our connection to You and the blessings of Your intimate companionship. May our spiritual journey be a testament to Your ceaseless love and mercy. Amen.

"For I will pour water on the thirsty land, and streams on the dry ground; I will pour out my Spirit on your offspring, and my blessing on your descendants." - Isaiah 44:3

Prayer Notes

___
___
___
___
___
___
___
___
___
___
___
___
___
___

63. Anger at God
Finding Healing and Understanding

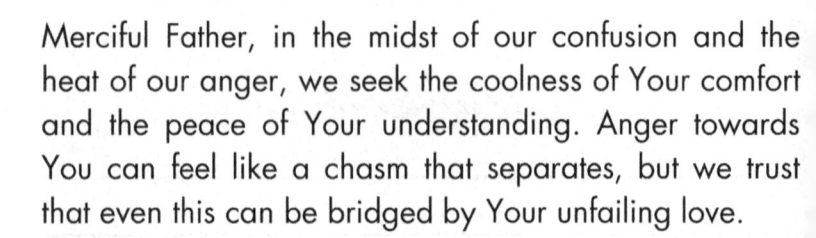

---♥---

Merciful Father, in the midst of our confusion and the heat of our anger, we seek the coolness of Your comfort and the peace of Your understanding. Anger towards You can feel like a chasm that separates, but we trust that even this can be bridged by Your unfailing love.

We lift up ourselves and others who bear the burden of frustration and misunderstanding in their hearts. Grant us the grace to navigate this stormy season with the compass of Your wisdom, transforming our anger into deeper insight and fellowship with You.

In the name of Jesus, our Great Mediator, we pray for healing from the wounds that spark our anger and a blessing of peace to soothe and restore our troubled spirits. Amen.

"Though he slay me, yet will I hope in him; I will surely defend my ways to his face." - Job 13:15

"My God, my God, why have you forsaken me? Why are you so far from saving me, so far from my cries of anguish? My God, I cry out by day, but you do not answer, by night, but I find no rest." - Psalm 22:1-2

Prayer Notes

64. Meaning of Suffering
Seeking Wisdom in Sorrow

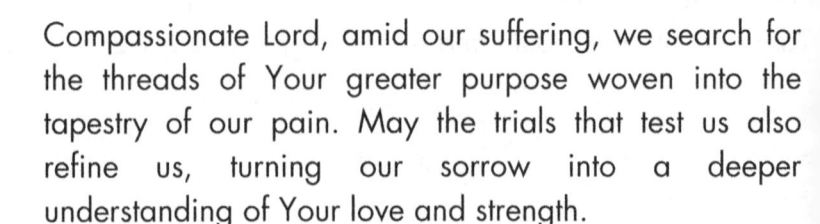

Compassionate Lord, amid our suffering, we search for the threads of Your greater purpose woven into the tapestry of our pain. May the trials that test us also refine us, turning our sorrow into a deeper understanding of Your love and strength.

For every heart that aches and soul that cries out in distress, we ask for the comfort of Your Spirit to embrace and sustain us. Instill the wisdom to see beyond the present hurt to the growth and compassion that can arise from our afflictions.

In the name of Jesus, our Great Comforter, we pray for the fortitude to endure and the insight to discern the lessons embedded within our struggles. Grant us the assurance that our current trials are a momentary preparation for eternal joy. Amen.

"I consider that our present sufferings are not worth comparing with the glory that will be revealed in us." - *Romans 8:18*

Prayer Notes

65. Alienation from the Religious Community

Building Community and Belonging

---- ♥ ----

Loving God, in the quiet corners of our hearts where loneliness echoes, we call out for the warmth of Your church, the body of Christ. In moments where we feel detached from our spiritual family, draw us nearer to the bond of fellowship that reflects Your love.

For all who wander outside the fold, who yearn for connection yet find themselves on the periphery, we seek Your guidance to open doors and build bridges. May we create spaces of welcome, understanding, and shared faith, living out the true meaning of Your community on Earth?

In the name of Jesus, our Great Unifier, we pray for unity and the blessing of belonging. Through Your divine grace, may we experience the inclusiveness of Your kingdom and embody the acceptance and love You offer. Amen.

"For I am convinced that neither death nor life, neither angels nor demons, neither the present nor the future, nor any powers, neither height nor depth, nor anything else in all creation, will be able to separate us from the love of God that is in Christ Jesus our Lord." - Romans 8:38-39

Prayer Notes

66. Ethical Dilemmas and Spiritual Integrity
Navigating Ethical Challenges

---♥---

O Wise and Just God, we seek Your light to illuminate our path in the labyrinth of life's ethical dilemmas. Guide us with Your wisdom so that we may discern right from wrong and uphold Your truth in our choices and actions.

For each soul facing the crossroads of decision, where moral clarity seems veiled in shades of gray, grant us the courage to choose integrity over convenience and righteousness over gain. Help us embody Your kingdom's principles, acting as beacons of justice and love in a world often guided by self-interest.

In the name of Jesus, our Great Guide, we pray for steadfastness in our ethical journey and Your blessing upon our endeavors to live out our faith with honor. May our lives reflect the depth of our commitment to You, navigating the complexities of morality with grace and strength. Amen.

"Blessed are those who hunger and thirst for righteousness, for they will be filled." - Matthew 5:6

Prayer Notes

---

67. Temptation and Spiritual Warfare

Resisting Temptation and Spiritual Battles

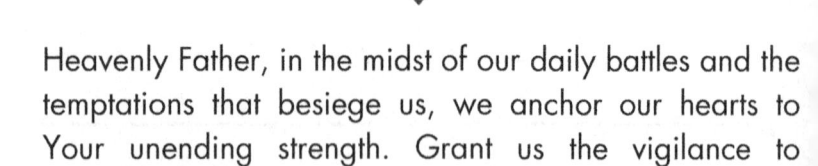

Heavenly Father, in the midst of our daily battles and the temptations that besiege us, we anchor our hearts to Your unending strength. Grant us the vigilance to recognize the snares laid before us and the wisdom to evade the allure of sin.

For ourselves and all who are engaged in the silent struggles of the spirit, we ask for a fortified will and a heart inclined towards Your goodness. Empower us to stand firm, clothed in the armor of faith, as we confront the challenges that test our resolve and dedication to Your path.

In the name of Jesus, our Great Protector, we pray for resilience in resisting temptation and for Your continued guidance and blessing in our spiritual warfare. May we emerge from these battles strengthened, not by our might, but through Your power and grace. Amen.

"No temptation has overtaken you except what is common to mankind. And God is faithful; he will not let you be tempted beyond what you can bear." - 1 Corinthians 10:13

Prayer Notes

---

68. Perseverance Through Trials
Enduring Strength in Trials

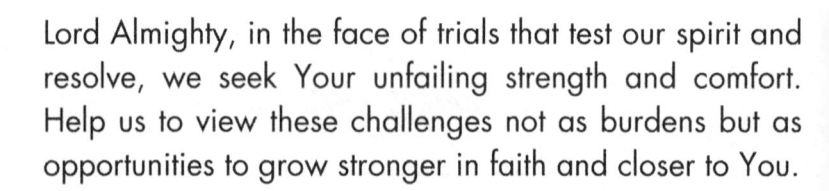

Lord Almighty, in the face of trials that test our spirit and resolve, we seek Your unfailing strength and comfort. Help us to view these challenges not as burdens but as opportunities to grow stronger in faith and closer to You.

For all who find themselves in the furnace of adversity, may we remember Your presence beside us, refining us like gold. Grant us the grace to persevere, to embrace each trial with courage, and to emerge not weary but fortified, with a deeper trust in Your plan and purpose.

In the name of Jesus, our Great Sustainer, we pray for endurance to withstand our trials and for Your continued dedication and blessing upon our journey. Let the resilience born of faith be our testament to Your enduring love and power. Amen.

"Consider it pure joy, my brothers and sisters, whenever you face trials of many kinds, because you know that the testing of your faith produces perseverance." - James 1:2-3

Prayer Notes

69. Perseverance Through Persecution

Resisting Temptation and Spiritual Battles

Heavenly Father, in the shadow of persecution for the sake of righteousness, we find strength in Your eternal promise. As we walk through the valley of misunderstanding and opposition, anchor our hearts to the truth of Your Word, empowering us to stand firm in our faith.

We pray that all who face the fire of persecution may be enveloped in Your protective grace and peace. May their spirits be unbreakable, their resolve unwavering, and their hearts steadfast in the assurance of Your love and approval.

In the name of Jesus, our Great Defender, we pray for resilience in the face of trials and for Your continued dedication and blessing upon those who persevere for righteousness' sake. May we embody the courage and faith that honors You, drawing ever closer to the promise of Your kingdom. Amen.

"Blessed are those who are persecuted because of righteousness, for theirs is the kingdom of heaven." - Matthew 5:10

Prayer Notes

70. Feelings of Unworthiness
Embracing Self-Worth and Grace

O God of all grace, in our moments of self-doubt and feelings of unworthiness, we are reminded of Your profound love for us. Help us to grasp the depth of Your mercy, which declares us worthy not by our deeds but by the sacrifice of Your Son.

For all burdened by self-condemnation, may Your Spirit lift our eyes to see ourselves as You see us: redeemed, called, and cherished. Instill the truth that our value is not earned but given freely through Your grace.

In the name of Jesus, our Great Redeemer, we pray for the embrace of our true identity as Your children and for the blessing of self-worth that flows from Your unending love. May we walk in the assurance that, in Your eyes, we are indeed enough. Amen.

"But God demonstrates his own love for us in this: While we were still sinners, Christ died for us." - Romans 5:8

"See what great love the Father has lavished on us, that we should be called children of God! And that is what we are!" - 1 John 3:1

Prayer Notes

71. Life Meaning and Purpose
Navigating Through Letdowns

Lord of Purpose, we seek Your guiding hand in our search for meaning amid life's letdowns. Remind us that our journey is not a string of random steps but a path designed by You, rich with intention and opportunity for growth.

For every soul wandering in the maze of disappointments, grant clarity that each experience and setback is a brushstroke in the masterpiece You are creating. Help us see your plan at work, molding us into vessels fit for your service and good works.

In the name of Jesus, our Great Director, we pray for insight into the unique purpose You have ordained for us and the strength to walk faithfully in it. Bless our days with Your presence so we may find joy and fulfillment in fulfilling Your will. Amen.

"For we are his workmanship, created in Christ Jesus for good works, which God prepared beforehand, that we should walk in them." - Ephesians 2:10

Prayer Notes

Part V:
Engaging the Present: Prayers for Contemporary Struggles

Introduction

In "Engaging the Present: Prayers for Contemporary Struggles," we enter a sanctuary of solace for the unique trials of our era. This section offers prayers that resonate with the pulse of modern life, addressing the whirlwind of digital engagement, the quiet epidemic of loneliness, and the pervasive unease for our planet's future.

As we navigate the complexities of economic, social, and environmental realities, these prayers are a call to spiritual arms. Here, we seek guidance in a world where progress often outpaces peace, and the sacred can be obscured by the urgent.

Through heartfelt petitions, we aim to reclaim balance and find clarity. These prayers are our companions in turning worries into wisdom, engaging with the present not just with our minds but with the resilient spirit of faith.

72. Information Overload
Seeking Clarity and Peace

Dear Heavenly Father, we seek Your clarity and peace in our world filled with endless information. Grant us wisdom to discern the essentials, guiding us toward Your truths and away from distractions. Help us focus on spiritual growth amidst the noise competing for our attention.

We ask for strength to navigate the deluge of news and digital demands. Instill in us tranquility and focus, allowing us to find rest in Your presence, as urged in Habakkuk 2:20. Remind us to be silent before Your holy temple. Teach us to quiet our minds, listen for Your voice, and find comfort in Your promises.

Bless us with patience as we strive for balance in this digital age, encouraging moments of reflection and deeper connection with You.

We pray for renewed dedication and peace in the name of Jesus, our Great Healer. Amen.

"But the Lord is in his holy temple; let all the earth be silent before him." - Habakkuk 2:20

Prayer Notes

73. Social Isolation
Cultivating Connections

--- ♥ ---

Heavenly Father, in these times of increasing social isolation, we reach out to You, seeking the warmth of Your love and guidance to forge meaningful connections. Infuse our hearts with courage and openness so that we might extend Your love to those around us, breaking through the barriers of loneliness and separation.

Empower us, Lord, to be beacons of Your light, using every opportunity to touch the lives of others with kindness, empathy, and understanding. Help us to recognize the silent struggles of those suffering in isolation and grant us the wisdom to offer support in ways that uplift and heal.

Strengthen our community bonds, Father, encouraging us to build bridges of friendship and solidarity. We pray for their continued dedication and blessing in the name of Jesus, our Great Healer. Amen.

"Be completely humble and gentle; be patient, bearing with one another in love." - Ephesians 4:2

Prayer Notes

74. Pace of Life
Discovering Stillness in a Fast-paced World

Gracious God, in the relentless rush of our daily lives, we seek Your sanctuary of peace and stillness. Teach us to slow down and embrace the moments of quiet that bring us closer to You. Help us understand the value of rest in our ceaseless quest for progress, reminding us that in stillness, there lies profound wisdom and renewal.

Guide our hearts to find a balance between action and reflection, Lord, ensuring that our spirits, bodies, and minds are nourished. Encourage us to seek Your presence in the pauses, finding joy and contentment in the simplicity of being rather than in constant doing.

In the pursuit of tranquility amidst turmoil, may we discover the strength and clarity that come from resting in You. In the name of Jesus, our Great Healer, we pray for their continued dedication and blessing. Amen.

"Be still, and know that I am God; I will be exalted among the nations, I will be exalted in the earth." - Psalm 46:10

Prayer Notes

---

75. Cyberbullying
Seeking Kindness in Digital Spaces

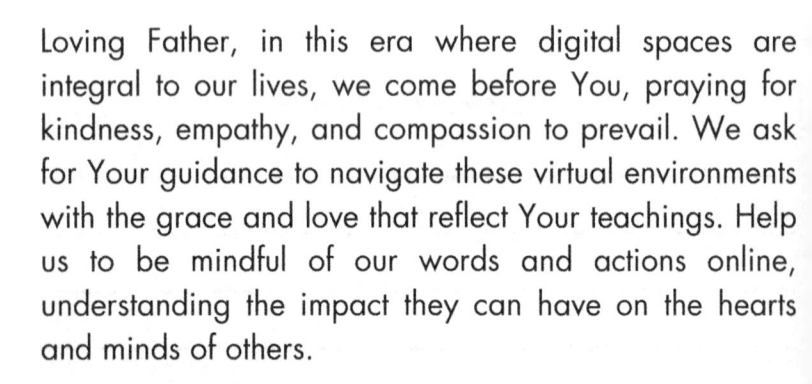

Loving Father, in this era where digital spaces are integral to our lives, we come before You, praying for kindness, empathy, and compassion to prevail. We ask for Your guidance to navigate these virtual environments with the grace and love that reflect Your teachings. Help us to be mindful of our words and actions online, understanding the impact they can have on the hearts and minds of others.

Grant us the strength to stand against cyberbullying, to be voices of support and encouragement in the face of hostility and negativity. May we create communities that are safe, inclusive, and reflective of Your unwavering love and acceptance. Help us remember the power of kindness, especially when we encounter or witness cyberbullying.

We look to You for inspiration and strength in our efforts to foster a kinder digital world. In the name of Jesus, our Great Healer, we pray for guidance and courage in promoting kindness and preventing harm. Amen.

"Let no corrupting talk come out of your mouths, but only such as is good for building up, as fits the occasion, that it may give grace to those who hear." - Ephesians 4:29

Prayer Notes

76. Mental Health Awareness
Fostering Understanding and Support

Heavenly Father, as we champion mental health understanding and support, we seek Your wisdom and fortitude. Enlighten us to perceive the battles faced by those around us, responding with empathy, aid, and kindness. Guide us to dismantle the stigmas enveloping mental health, fostering an environment of open conversation and acceptance.

Empower us with insight to provide solace and bravery to demand better resources and support for the silent sufferers. Instruct us in attentive listening, fostering a community where all feel seen, heard, and uplifted.

We petition for Your direction and blessings in this mission of mental health enlightenment. In the name of Jesus, our Great Healer, we ask for the light to guide our path and unwavering commitment to empathy and aid. Amen.

"Bear one another's burdens, and so fulfill the law of Christ." - Galatians 6:2.

Prayer Notes

77. Burnout
Restoring Balance and Well-being

Almighty God, in the midst of our exhaustion and burnout, we seek Your rejuvenating presence. Teach us the importance of rest and stepping back to replenish our spirits. Help us to recognize the signs of burnout in ourselves and others, offering the support and understanding needed to restore balance and well-being.

Guide us, Lord, in establishing boundaries that protect our time and energy, enabling us to serve You and those around us with renewed passion and dedication. Instill in us the wisdom to prioritize self-care as an act of faith, trusting that in our well-being, we are better equipped to reflect Your love and compassion in the world.

In our journey towards recovery and balance, we lean on Your everlasting strength. In the name of Jesus, our Great Healer, we pray for resilience and renewal in our dedication to care for ourselves and others. Amen.

"Come to me, all who labor and are heavy laden, and I will give you rest." - Matthew 11:28

Prayer Notes

---

78. Economic Insecurity

Finding Financial Peace

Heavenly Father, we seek Your wisdom and guidance in times of economic insecurity and financial uncertainty. Help us navigate these challenging waters with faith and prudence, trusting in Your provision. Teach us to manage our resources wisely, be generous despite our fears, and remember that our security ultimately lies not in wealth but in Your steadfast love.

Encourage us, Lord, to support one another in need, fostering a community of care and sharing that reflects Your generosity. Inspire us to find creative solutions to our financial challenges, and grant us the peace that transcends understanding, knowing You are with us in every circumstance.

We pray for Your guidance and blessing as we seek financial peace and stability. In the name of Jesus, our Great Healer, we pray for wisdom and courage in our journey toward economic security and financial stewardship. Amen.

"But seek first his kingdom and his righteousness, and all these things will be given to you as well." - Matthew 6:33

Prayer Notes

79. Overconsumption and Materialism

Embracing Simplicity and Contentment

Gracious God, in a world where overconsumption and materialism often overshadow the essence of true happiness, we seek Your guidance to embrace simplicity and contentment. Help us recognize the fleeting nature of material possessions and find joy in the abundance of Your creation. Teach us to appreciate the beauty of simplicity, the value of restraint, and the peace that comes from being content with what we have.

Inspire us, Lord, to lead lives that reflect Your priorities, focusing on relationships, generosity, and service rather than the accumulation of goods. Encourage us to support one another in our journey towards a more meaningful existence, free from the chains of consumerism.

We pray for Your wisdom and grace as we strive to live more simply and contentedly. In the name of Jesus, our Great Healer, we pray for the strength to resist the temptations of materialism and the courage to embrace a life of true fulfillment and blessing. Amen.

"Keep your life free from love of money, and be content with what you have, for He has said, 'I will never leave you nor forsake you.'" - *Hebrews 13:5*

Prayer Notes

80. Work-Life Imbalance
Seeking Harmony and Fulfillment

Lord Almighty, in the midst of our struggle with work-life imbalance, we seek Your guidance to find harmony and fulfillment. Teach us to set boundaries that honor our professional commitments and our need for rest, relationships, and personal growth. Help us to prioritize our time and energy in a way that reflects what truly matters, fostering a balance that nurtures our whole being.

Give us the wisdom to recognize when work overshadows our life and the courage to make changes that align with Your will for our well-being and happiness. Encourage us, Father, to support one another in this journey, sharing our struggles and victories so that we might find strength and inspiration in our shared experiences.

In the name of Jesus, our Great Healer, we pray for the perseverance and insight needed to achieve harmony and fulfillment in all our lives. Amen.

"For everything there is a season, and a time for every matter under heaven." - Ecclesiastes 3:1

Prayer Notes

---

81. Parenting Challenges
Guiding with Wisdom and Patience

Heavenly Father, in the face of parenting challenges, we come to You seeking wisdom and patience. Guide us to raise our children with love, understanding, and firmness that reflects Your care for us. Help us to listen with empathy, discipline with kindness, and model the values we wish to instill in them.

Grant us the insight to recognize the unique gifts You have placed in each of our children and the wisdom to nurture those gifts according to Your will. Let our homes be places of joy, learning, and peace, where Your presence is felt in every interaction.

As we navigate the complexities of parenting, we lean on Your everlasting strength. In the name of Jesus, we pray for the grace to guide our children with wisdom and patience, making decisions that foster their growth into compassionate and resilient individuals. Amen.

"Train up a child in the way he should go; even when he is old he will not depart from it." - Proverbs 22:6

Prayer Notes

82. Single Parenting
Affirming Strength and Support

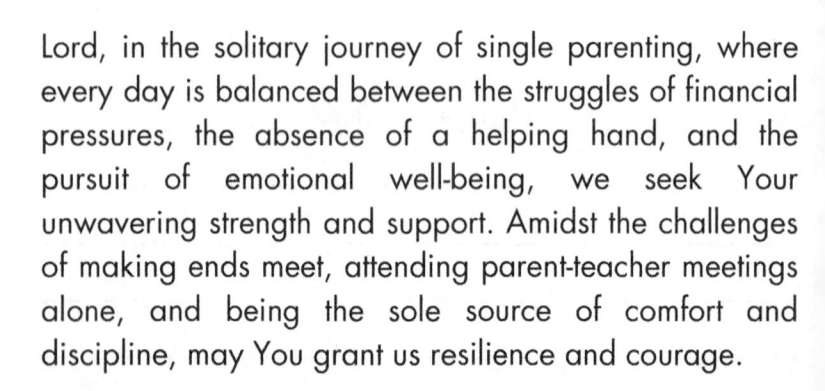

Lord, in the solitary journey of single parenting, where every day is balanced between the struggles of financial pressures, the absence of a helping hand, and the pursuit of emotional well-being, we seek Your unwavering strength and support. Amidst the challenges of making ends meet, attending parent-teacher meetings alone, and being the sole source of comfort and discipline, may You grant us resilience and courage.

Bless us with a community that uplifts and supports us, mirroring Your love and compassion. May we find solace in Your presence during moments of doubt and fatigue, remembering that we are never truly alone with You.

As we navigate the challenges and triumphs of single parenting, we rest in Your grace and provision. In the name of Jesus, our Great Healer, we pray for continued strength and blessing in our commitment to raising our children. Amen.

"My grace is sufficient for you, for my power is made perfect in weakness." - 2 Corinthians 12:9

Prayer Notes

---

83. Negative Influences
Seeking Positive Paths

Heavenly Father, in a world where negative influences often cloud our judgment and lead us astray, we turn to You for guidance and protection. Help us discern the paths that align with Your will, resist the temptations that lead to harm, and embrace the actions and thoughts that reflect Your goodness and love.

Empower us, Lord, to stand firm against the pressures and influences that seek to divert us from Your purpose. Fill our hearts with Your light so that we may be beacons of positivity and hope in our communities, influencing others towards paths of righteousness and peace.

As we navigate the challenges of negative influences, we seek Your wisdom and guidance. In the name of Jesus, we pray for the courage and conviction to choose positive paths and the continued dedication and blessing of all who walk in Your light. Amen.

"Do not be overcome by evil, but overcome evil with good." - Romans 12:21

Prayer Notes

84. Privacy and Surveillance
Protecting Privacy and Dignity

Lord, in this era where privacy and surveillance challenge the core of our dignity, we come before You, seeking wisdom and protection. Help us to navigate this digital age with discernment, ensuring that our actions honor the privacy and dignity of ourselves and others. Guide those in positions of power to use technology responsibly, valuing the individual rights and freedoms You have bestowed upon us.

Grant us the courage to speak out against invasions of privacy and the insight to protect our personal spaces from undue scrutiny. May we foster a society that respects boundaries and cherishes the sanctity of individuality as part of Your divine creation?

As we seek to balance technological advancements with ethical considerations, we pray for Your guidance and grace. In the name of Jesus, we pray for the perseverance to safeguard our privacy and dignity and for the blessing of wisdom in all who influence the surveillance landscape. Amen.

"For you created my inmost being; you knit me together in my mother's womb. I praise you because I am fearfully and wonderfully made; your works are wonderful, I know that full well." - Psalm 139:13-14

Prayer Notes

---

85. Cultural Conflict
Building Bridges of Understanding

Heavenly Father, in a world marked by cultural conflict and misunderstanding, we seek Your guidance to build bridges of understanding and empathy. Teach us to celebrate the diversity of Your creation, recognizing the beauty in our differences and the strength in our unity. Help us approach each interaction with open hearts and minds, ready to learn from one another and share Your love and grace.

Empower us, Lord, to be peacemakers in our communities, using our words and actions to foster dialogue, respect, and reconciliation. May we be instruments of Your peace, breaking down walls of division and building pathways of mutual respect and understanding.

As we work towards a world where every culture is valued, and every individual is seen as a reflection of Your image, we pray for Your wisdom and strength. In the name of Jesus, we pray for the commitment and blessing of all involved in this journey toward harmony and understanding. Amen.

"If it is possible, as far as it depends on you, live at peace with everyone." - Romans 12:18

Prayer Notes

86. Authentic Connections
Deepening Bonds in a Superficial Age

Heavenly Father, in this age, where superficial connections often replace genuine relationships, we come to You longing for authenticity and depth in our interactions. Guide us to cultivate true connections that reflect Your love and grace, relationships rooted in honesty, empathy, and mutual respect. Help us prioritize meaningful communication, listen deeply, and share our true selves with others.

Grant us the courage to be vulnerable, to open our hearts in a way that fosters genuine bonds and understanding. Strengthen us to build communities where authentic connections thrive, shining as beacons of Your light in a world craving real intimacy and fellowship.

We seek Your wisdom for deeper, authentic relationships. In Jesus' name, we pray for the dedication to nurture meaningful bonds that mirror Your intent for us. Amen.

"Therefore, as God's chosen people, holy and dearly loved, clothe yourselves with compassion, kindness, humility, gentleness and patience." - Colossians 3:12

Prayer Notes

87. Environmental Grief
Fostering Hope and Action

Creator God, as we face the growing challenges of environmental degradation, we come to You with heavy hearts, feeling the weight of what we have lost. Yet, in this grief, we seek solace and the strength to act. Guide us to be stewards of Your creation, inspiring us to protect and restore the Earth for future generations. Help us to find hope amidst despair, channeling our grief into meaningful action that honors Your creation.

Empower us, Lord, with the courage to change our lives and advocate for policies that safeguard the environment. Inspire us to work together, across divides, in our common goal of healing the planet. May our actions reflect our responsibility to You and all who call this world home.

We ask for your guidance and blessing in pursuing a healthier, more sustainable world. In the name of Jesus, our Great Healer, we pray for the dedication to continue our efforts and the blessing of hope to sustain us in our journey. Amen.

"The earth is the Lord's, and everything in it, the world, and all who live in it;" - Psalm 24:1

Prayer Notes

88. Obesity
Nurturing Health and Wholeness

Lord, in our journey towards overcoming obesity, we seek Your guidance and strength. Help us cultivate a lifestyle that honors the body You have given us, one that is rooted in balance, health, and respect for ourselves. Inspire us to make choices each day that lead to wholeness, not just in body but also in spirit and mind.

Grant us the wisdom to understand the complexities of obesity, compassion for those who struggle with it, and the determination to support one another in our paths to better health. Provide us with the resources and support needed to make sustainable changes, fostering environments that promote physical well-being and emotional resilience.

In this pursuit of health and wholeness, we lean on Your love and strength. In the name of Jesus, our Great Healer, we pray for the dedication to nurture our bodies and spirits and the blessing of renewed health and vitality for all. Amen.

"Do you not know that your bodies are temples of the Holy Spirit, who is in you, whom you have received from God? You are not your own;" - 1 Corinthians 6:19

Prayer Notes

89. Travel Safety
Praying for Mercy and Protection

Heavenly Father, as we embark on our journeys, both near and far, we seek Your mercy and protection. Surround us with Your loving care on every road and in every mode of travel. Guard us against the dangers of the way; keep us alert, preserve us from harm, and guide us safely to our destinations.

Instill in us a spirit of wisdom and caution that we may make decisions that ensure not only our safety but also the safety of those around us. Help us to be mindful of Your presence, trusting in Your providence to lead us through every journey.

In our coming and going, we rely on Your grace and protection. In the name of Jesus, we pray for the dedication to travel wisely and for the blessing of safety and peace on all our travels. Amen.

"The Lord will keep you from all harm—he will watch over your life; the Lord will watch over your coming and going both now and forevermore." - Psalm 121:7-8

Prayer Notes

90. Healthcare Access
Seeking Healing for All

Merciful God, as we confront the challenges of healthcare access, we come to You with hearts full of hope, seeking Your guidance and provision. Illuminate our paths so that we may find ways to extend healing and support to all, especially the most vulnerable among us. Inspire those in positions of power to create systems that ensure everyone can receive the care they need, reflecting Your compassion and justice.

Grant wisdom to healthcare professionals, caregivers, and policymakers so that they might work together to remove barriers to access, making healthcare not a privilege but a right for everyone. Help us remember the value of each life, encouraging us to advocate for equitable solutions that honor the dignity of all Your children.

In our efforts to create a more inclusive healthcare system, we lean on Your strength and wisdom. In the name of Jesus, we pray for the dedication to healing the sick and for the blessing of accessible healthcare for all. Amen.

"He heals the brokenhearted and binds up their wounds." - Psalm 147:3

Prayer Notes

91. Educational Disparity
Equalizing Opportunities for Learning

Lord of all wisdom, we seek Your justice and guidance in the face of educational disparities. Open our eyes to the inequalities that hinder many from accessing the learning they deserve. Inspire us, and those with the power to make a difference, to work tirelessly towards an education system that is inclusive, equitable, and reflective of Your kingdom, where every child has the opportunity to learn and grow.

Empower educators, policymakers, and communities to break down disparity barriers, innovate, and create environments where all students can thrive, regardless of their background. Instill a spirit of solidarity and compassion to support one another in pursuing knowledge and understanding.

In our efforts to foster educational equity, we pray for Your wisdom and strength. In the name of Jesus, our Great Healer, we pray for the dedication to equalize learning opportunities and the blessing of all students' enlightenment and growth. Amen.

"Learn to do right; seek justice. Defend the oppressed. Take up the cause of the fatherless; plead the case of the widow." - Isaiah 1:17

Prayer Notes

92. Elderly Care
Honoring and Supporting Seniors

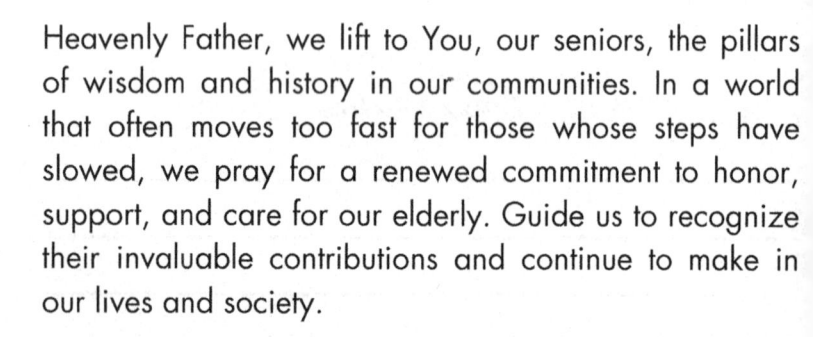

Heavenly Father, we lift to You, our seniors, the pillars of wisdom and history in our communities. In a world that often moves too fast for those whose steps have slowed, we pray for a renewed commitment to honor, support, and care for our elderly. Guide us to recognize their invaluable contributions and continue to make in our lives and society.

Help us ensure that they are cared for with dignity and respect and cherished and engaged as integral members of our communities. Provide strength and patience to professional and familial caregivers, imbuing them with Your love and compassion. May we create environments that foster connection, respect their autonomy, and meet their physical, emotional, and spiritual needs.

In our service to the elderly, we seek Your grace and guidance. In the name of Jesus, our Great Healer, we pray for the dedication to advocate for and support our seniors, ensuring they feel valued and loved. Amen.

"Honor your father and mother"—which is the first commandment with a promise—"so that it may go well with you and that you may enjoy long life on the earth."
- Ephesians 6:2-3

Prayer Notes

93. Racism and Inequality
Pursuing Equity and Empathy

Lord of all creation, in a world marred by racism and inequality, we come to You seeking the courage to confront these injustices and the wisdom to heal the divisions they cause. Teach us to love as You love, without prejudice or condition, recognizing every person's inherent dignity and worth created in Your image.

Instill in us a deep sense of empathy and understanding so that we might listen to the experiences of those who suffer discrimination and stand alongside them in their struggle for justice and equality. Empower us to be agents of change in our communities, advocating for policies and practices that promote equity and dismantle the structures of oppression that have long divided us.

We pray for Your guidance and strength in our journey towards a more just and compassionate world. In the name of Jesus, we pray for the dedication to pursue equity and the blessing of empathy to bridge the gaps of understanding among us. Amen.

"There is neither Jew nor Gentile, neither slave nor free, nor is there male and female, for you are all one in Christ Jesus." - Galatians 3:28

Prayer Notes

94. Political Division
Fostering Civic Harmony

---♥---

Heavenly Father, in these times of deep political division, we seek Your wisdom and grace to navigate the complexities of our civic responsibilities with love and respect. Guide us towards understanding and harmony, encouraging dialogue that bridges divides rather than widening them. Help us to remember that, above all, we are Your children, called to love one another despite our differences.

Inspire leaders and citizens to prioritize the common good, making just, compassionate decisions that reflect Your will for peace and unity. Give us the courage to listen, the humility to learn, and the strength to work together to better our communities and nation.

As we strive for civic harmony, we lean on Your eternal guidance. In Jesus' name, we pray for the dedication to seek common ground and for the blessing of peace in our hearts and among our people. Amen.

"Blessed are the peacemakers, for they will be called children of God." - Matthew 5:9

Prayer Notes

95. Violence
Cultivating Peace and Safety

Lord of Peace, in a world where violence seems ever-present, we come to You with heavy hearts, yearning for Your peace and protection. Help us be instruments of Your peace, actively cultivating safe environments for all people. Inspire us to spread love where there is hatred, to offer healing where there is injury, and to sow unity in places of division.

Grant wisdom and courage to those in positions of authority to implement just policies that protect the vulnerable and promote peace. Strengthen our communities to stand together against violence, supporting one another in times of fear and distress. May we embody Your compassion and mercy in our actions and interactions.

As we seek a world where peace prevails over violence, we ask for Your guiding hand. In the name of Jesus, we pray for the dedication to create and maintain safety for all and the blessing of a lasting peace that comforts every heart. Amen.

"Turn from evil and do good; seek peace and pursue it."
- Psalm 34:14

Prayer Notes

96. Poverty
Eradicating Hunger and Need

Heavenly Provider, in a world where poverty afflicts so many, leaving countless individuals and families in hunger and need, we lift our hearts to You, praying for Your intervention and guidance. Inspire us, Your children, to act with compassion and urgency to address the root causes of poverty and to meet the immediate needs of the hungry and the deprived.

Empower us to share our resources generously, to advocate for just economic systems, and to support initiatives that provide sustainable solutions to poverty. Open our eyes to see the dignity and worth of every person, driving us to act in love and solidarity.

In our efforts to eradicate hunger and need, we seek Your wisdom and strength. In the name of Jesus, we pray for the dedication to serve those in poverty and for the blessing of a world where every person can live in dignity and abundance. Amen.

"For I was hungry and you gave me something to eat, I was thirsty and you gave me something to drink, I was a stranger and you invited me in," - Matthew 25:35.

Prayer Notes

97. Homelessness
Advocating Shelter and Community

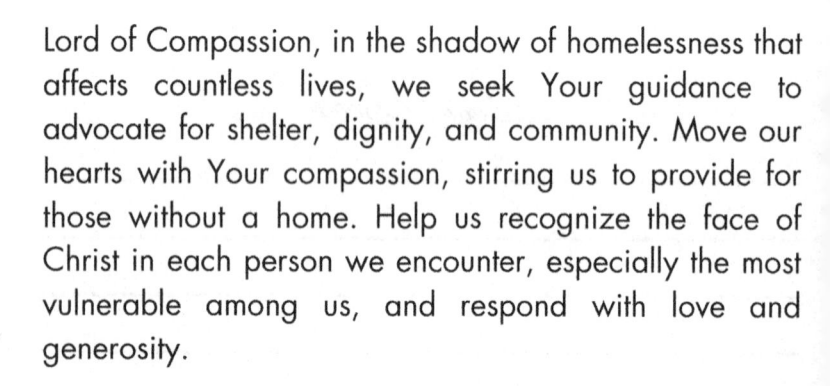

Lord of Compassion, in the shadow of homelessness that affects countless lives, we seek Your guidance to advocate for shelter, dignity, and community. Move our hearts with Your compassion, stirring us to provide for those without a home. Help us recognize the face of Christ in each person we encounter, especially the most vulnerable among us, and respond with love and generosity.

Inspire us to support initiatives that offer temporary shelter and pathways to stable, long-term housing and reintegration into community life. Encourage policymakers, organizations, and individuals to collaborate in creating solutions that address the root causes of homelessness, ensuring everyone has access to safe and affordable housing.

As we aim to eradicate homelessness, we seek Your strength and wisdom. In Jesus' name, we pray for dedication in aiding those without homes and for community support to uplift and empower all in need. Amen.

"There will always be poor people in the land. Therefore I command you to be openhanded toward your fellow Israelites who are poor and needy in your land." - Deuteronomy 15:11

Prayer Notes

98. Fatherlessness
Embracing the Orphaned with Love

Heavenly Father, we bring before You children growing up without fathers. Fill their lives with Your love and guidance, and inspire us to act as Your instruments of support and mentorship for them.

Motivate our communities to provide the stability and encouragement these children need. Let Your church be a home and beacon of hope for the fatherless, showcasing Your love for them as Psalm 68:5-6a reminds us, 'A father to the fatherless, a defender of widows, is God in his holy dwelling.'

Equip us with Your compassion and wisdom as we commit to supporting and uplifting the orphaned. In the name of Jesus, our Great Healer, we pray for the strength to pursue this mission and the transformative power of love to change lives. Amen.

"A father to the fatherless, a defender of widows, is God in his holy dwelling. God sets the lonely in families, he leads out the prisoners with singing..." - Psalm 68:5-6a

Prayer Notes

99. Human Trafficking
Championing Freedom and Recovery

Lord of Justice and Mercy, we cry out to You on behalf of the countless lives ensnared by the chains of human trafficking. Illuminate the darkness with Your light, bringing hope and freedom to those suffering under this grave injustice. Empower us, Your followers, to be vigilant defenders of human dignity, actively working to end this exploitation.

Guide and strengthen those who are on the front lines fighting against trafficking, from law enforcement to advocates and survivors leading the charge for change. Provide comfort and healing to victims, restoring their spirits and rebuilding their lives on the foundation of Your love.

As we strive to champion freedom and recovery for all affected by human trafficking, we ask for Your guidance and protection. In the name of Jesus, our Great Healer, we pray for the dedication to eradicate this evil and for the blessing of renewed strength and hope for every soul touched by trafficking. Amen.

"He has sent me to bind up the brokenhearted, to proclaim freedom for the captives and release from darkness for the prisoners," - Isaiah 61:1

Prayer Notes

100. Justice
Upholding Righteousness in the Present

Sovereign Lord, in a world where injustice often prevails, we turn to You, seeking Your wisdom and strength to uphold righteousness. Guide us to act justly, love mercifully, and walk humbly with You as we reflect Your justice daily. Empower us to advocate for the oppressed, speak out against wrongdoing, and support systems and policies that promote equity and fairness.

Strengthen our resolve to work for justice in our communities, inspiring others to join this holy calling. May our actions be a testament to Your unending love and commitment to righteousness. Help us to navigate the complexities of the present age with discernment and courage, always aiming to embody the principles of Your kingdom.

As we strive for justice, we seek Your guidance and grace. In the name of Jesus, our Great Healer, we pray for the dedication to uphold righteousness and the blessing of a more just and compassionate world. Amen.

"But when you ask, you must believe and not doubt, because the one who doubts is like a wave of the sea, blown and tossed by the wind." - James 1:6
"I believe; help my unbelief!" - Mark 9:24

Prayer Notes

Made in United States
North Haven, CT
15 August 2024